A Complete Guide to Wills, Trusts and Estate Planning

JOSEPH R. BURCKE

Copyright © 2014 Joseph R. Burcke

All rights reserved. No part of this book may be reproduced or transmitted in any form or by any means, electronic or mechanical, including photocopying, recording or by any information storage and retrieval system, without the express written consent of the author, except for the inclusion of brief quotations in a review.

Published by Joseph R. Burcke, L.L.C.
7777 Bonhomme Ave., Suite 1501
St. Louis, Missouri 63105
All rights reserved.

ISBN: 1495457478
ISBN-13:978149547470

Library of Congress Control Number: 2014903938

Burcke, Joseph R.

A Guide to Wills, Trusts, and estate Planning: Everything You Always Wanted to Know But Were Afraid to Ask.

DEDICATION

This book is dedicated to those many kind attorneys who have provided me with professional and personal guidance over the years. Law schools teach students how to "think like a lawyer" but don't really teach how to practice law in the real world. I was fortunate to have many attorneys and judges my senior take the time and make the effort to help me practice law with honor and dignity. I owe these men and women gratitude and dedicate this book to them. Finally, a word of thanks to my ever astute editor who has consistently warned me against the use of semi colons throughout.

CONTENTS

Acknowledgments

Introduction — i

1. What Constitutes an Estate — 6
2. What is a Trust and How Does it Work? — 16
3. What is so bad about Probate Anyway? — 30
4. The Most Common Planning Options — 51
5. Estate Taxation, The Basics — 68
6. Retirement Benefits are Beneficiary Designations Enough? — 75
7. Planning for the Disabled Beneficiary — 86
8. Planning for Your Own Disability NAME — 98
9. How To Choose Your Estate Planning Attorney — 115
10. Making the Most of Your Planning Conference — 145

Appendices — 157

    Estate Taxation, The Basics — 159

    The Marital Deduction Trust And Marital Planning — 173

    Some Sophisticate Estate Tax Planning Strategies — 191

Chapter One

What Constitutes an Estate?

The first concept to be discussed is that of "the estate". While the most elementary of all estate planning concepts, even here we can see the complexity of the subject matter. Each person alive potentially has two estates, not one, to consider when planning; the "probate" estate and the "estate taxable" estate.

The Probate Estate:

Let's start with the simpler of the two. Whenever you see the word "probate", the next word that should immediately pop into your mind is the word "title". The reason probate processes exist is to solve a simple, yet important problem:

PROBATE=TITLE

Due to the disability or death of a title holder of an asset, the title holder, literally, cannot sign his or her own name. Because of this inability, nothing can be done with the asset. It cannot be legally sold, bartered, mortgaged or otherwise pledged or conveyed because the title owner cannot evidence his or her consent to the transaction.

Why?

Because he or she cannot sign his or her name to the commercial document evidencing the transaction.

The whole purpose of probate, in a conservatorship (where the genesis of the inability to sign is disability,) and decedent estate proceedings (where death causes such inability,) is to provide a legal process that affords a substitute for the title holder and provides such substitute the legal ability to sign the title holder's name when he or she cannot; The conservator of the conservatorship and the executor or personal representative in the case of a decedent estate.

The purpose of probate is to provide a key to unlock titles to assets which have become "locked up" as a result of the owner's inability to sign his own name.

In determining what assets will be subjected to probate upon disability or death, one simply looks to how the title is held. If one is the sole title owner of the asset, a title holder with others as a tenant in common, or if one is the last surviving joint title holder, at one's death the asset must be probated. Upon one's disability, with a few exceptions to be later noted, even if one has other joint tenants still alive and holding title with him or her; there will still need to be a conservatorship, to "unlock" the asset whose title has been "locked" up because of disability.

Thus, this rule holds true for most of the assets we all tend to own: real estate, depository accounts (savings accounts, checking accounts and many money market accounts), stocks, bonds, C.D.s, motor vehicles, and personalty.

But what about other, more complex assets?

What about life insurance? If you are the owner/insured of a life insurance policy, the odds are fairly good that the insurance policy will be excluded from your probate estate. A life insurance policy is actually a contract, between you and the insurance company. According to the terms of that contract, in return for your premium payment, the insurer promises at your death to pay the proceeds of the policy to the person(s) or entities whom you have designated as beneficiaries of the policy. Because, under the terms of the contract, the insurer is obligated to pay the policy proceeds directly to the designated beneficiary, the policy proceeds pass "outside" of probate at the insured's death.

On the other hand, if there is a failure of designation of a death beneficiary (the beneficiary dies before the owner/insured life) then one has to look to the terms of the policy itself to determine whether or not the policy proceeds will be a probatable asset at the death of the insured/owner. Many policies have a default provision identifying by blood relationship the individual to whom the insurer is obligated to pay the policy proceeds in case of a failure of designation of beneficiary.

Many policies' default provision provides that the policy proceeds, in the absence of a named beneficiary, are payable to the owner/insured's estate; in which case, the policy proceeds are included in the title holders probate estate at death. If you are the owner of an insurance policy insuring the life of someone other than yourself, should you die before the insured life, the life insurance policy is includable in your probate estate and its value is determined by the cash value, if any, built up in the policy as of the date of your death, less any loan value outstanding against the policy.

What about so called deferred benefit assets; pensions, profit sharing plans, IRAs 401 ks and the like? Is the value of these assets included in a plan participant's probate estate at the time of his or her death? The most likely answer is NO. Like insurance policies, the underlying nature of the asset is a contractual obligation to pay a designated third party or parties at the death of the plan participant. However, even if the designated beneficiary predeceases the plan participant, the value of the asset will be excluded from the participant's probatable estate. Federal law precludes provision in the contracts that underlay such retirement benefits of a return of the benefit to the plan participant's probate estate. Instead these plans will make provision for a scheme of inheritance within the plan provisions.

The Taxable Estate:

If you think the preceding was difficult, the horror has just begun. Whereas the controlling factor for the determination of probate was the identity of title holder, the controlling factors for determination of estate taxability include a much more difficult concept: incidences of ownership.

The tax code creates an "Alice in Wonderland" like world where the actuality of something is not really determinative of its treatment. Rather, it is the appearance of ownership like qualities that control whether an asset is includible in one's estate taxable estate, no matter the actual title ownership. Appearance of ownership is determined by the incidences of ownership which one has over an asset at the time of one's death. Even if not the title owner, if one has sufficient incidences of ownership, the asset will be included in the individual's taxable estate.

What are these incidences of ownership? They come in all shapes and sizes. For the sake of brevity and clarity of understanding, let's distill them down to their most basic essences. I believe that there are four basic incidences of ownership.

BASIC INCIDENCES OF OWNERSHIP

- Consumer use of the asset;
- Consumer use of income generated by the asset;
- Power to direct recipient of asset after one's death;
 (Power of Appointment)
- Investment control of the asset.

Under the provisions of the federal estate tax code, if you hold sufficient incidences of ownership, the tax code will deem you to be the owner even though you do not hold title to the asset in question.

What are the combinations of incidences that will cause inclusion of an asset in one's taxable estate?

Ah! Were it so easy as to have a formula or identifying quotient. However, there is no such absolute definition.

The law has developed on a case-by-case basis. While we can certainly identify certain combinations and degrees of incidences as causing inclusion; the list is ever developing by IRS interpretation and Tax Court decision. It is impossible to list all of the variations and conclude the list exhausted of additional possibilities. Besides, this book is supposed to be a general guide and not a scholarly effort of epic proportions; so I shall fail to include a combinations' list for easy reference.

Rather, let's look at the assets which we previously discussed when defining the concept of the probate estate to illuminate some differences of nuance.

Obviously, if one is the title owner of an asset, rest assured that the asset will be includible in one's taxable estate.

What about those less obvious assets like life insurance and retirement benefits?

With these types of assets, even if you are not the title holder, their value is still includible in your taxable estate if you have sufficient incidences of ownership.

For example, a trust (or even another person) can be the title owner of a life insurance policy; yet, if you have the power to direct the beneficiary; the power to direct the consumer enjoyment of the income; or the power to direct the investment of the value of the policy coupled with the right to enjoy the income or capital value of the policy (through a borrowing power, for instance), at death, the value of the policy is includible in your taxable estate.

What is the value includible in your taxable estate?

Many people incorrectly assume that the value included is the cash surrender value. Thus, many people ignore the value of term insurance when determining the value of their estate for estate tax purposes. To ignore the value of term insurance will always prove to be a costly mistake. The value includible in one's taxable estate is the face value of the policy, plus the value of any paid up additions less the value of any loans outstanding against the policy at the time of death. Thus a $100,000 term life insurance policy that is includible in one's taxable estate is worth $100,000 for estate tax purposes, although, absent death, the value of the policy in real life is considered zero.

The same holds true for deferred benefit assets.

Though an employee or retiree is not the owner of the company-sponsored retirement benefit, because he or she has the right to enjoy the income, possibly the principal (depending upon the type of plan) and can designate a death beneficiary who is entitled to receive the benefit of the retirement program after the plan participant's death; the value of the deferred benefit asset is includible in the plan participant's taxable estate.

What value is includible in your taxable estate?

It depends upon the type of benefit plan. If the retirement benefit is an IRA, invested in a CD, the computation is rather simple. The value is the principal and interest accrued as of the date of death. For defined benefit plans with a death beneficiary designation feature, the computation of value can be more complex. (I'll leave that to your accountant or plan administrator's determination.

CONCLUSION:

If you have kept a tally as to the identity and approximate value of your assets, one of life's unfortunate occurrences is that you are never quite so wealthy as at the moment of your death. An equally unfortunate life occurrence is that, in addition to your loved ones, there are entities interested in the nature and value of your estate. These are your unintended beneficiaries (absent competent planning): the state probate court process and the IRS.

Chapter Two
What is a Trust and How Does it Work?

Most people who come to my seminars do so to find out about living trusts. By now, almost everyone in America has heard about trusts in some form or other and believes them to be beneficial.

Few people, however, understand the structure of a trust; how a trust operates; and, most important, why it protects family wealth accumulation.

So, without further adieu, let's talk about trusts.

The first point to be made is that there is more than one kind of trust available to estate planners. Each type has different attributes and is used for different purposes by the planner. In this chapter we will look at the most basic type of trust which is the cornerstone of almost any basic estate plan: the Revocable Living Trust.

Revocable Living Trusts

A Revocable *Living* Trust, as that term is most commonly used, refers to a trust made during the creator's lifetime which takes effect upon its creation and funding. This is as opposed to a trust contained inside a Last Will and Testament which is called a *testamentary* trust which is not funded or takes effect until after the creator of the trust has died. The term *Revocable* means that if the creator of the trust is alive, the terms of the trust can be changed by its creator. If the creator so desires, the trust can even be revoked.

Another important attribute of this basic trust is that it is income tax neutral under both state and federal law. In other words, you get the same income tax treatment as if you had never created the trust and still held title to your assets in your sole name. You will still file a 1040 and comparable state income tax return and receive the same income tax treatment. In the Internal Revenue Code these income tax neutral trusts are called *Grantor* trusts, because the creator of the trust (the Grantor) for income tax purposes, is attributed the income tax consequences of the investment activity which takes place in the trust.

Trust Structure

To understand the basic structure of a trust, and to explain same to anyone else (just in case you, upon reading this book, decide to join the seminar circuit or wish to impress your friends at parties) you need only refer to the following simple diagram:

The Square

Think of the square as a box and the box as a treasure chest. (Seeing the drawing, you can understand why I didn't try to draw a treasure chest). The treasure chest is the trust itself, into which one puts substantially all of his/her family's assets.

How does one put assets into the treasure chest? The answer is quite simple; by *re-titling the assets* from the individual's name into the name of the trust. Regardless whether the titles to your assets are held in your sole name, jointly with others, or in common with others, you re-title such assets into the name of the trust.

Living Trust Planning is a two step process:

☐ Creation of the Trust Contract;

☐ Integration of Assets into the Trust.

How difficult is it to put your assets into the trust?

If you can remember your name and the words "Living Trust"; you can re-title any asset from yourself into the name of your trust.

Are all assets re-titled into the trust's name?

No. While it is relatively simple, as a mechanical process, to re-title assets, the decision about which assets to re-title is a bit more complex. This aspect (and the drafting of appropriate trust language to accomplish your desires) is best left to an estate planning attorney. In other words:

Kids, don't attempt to perform this trick at home. It takes a trained professional with years of experience to safely perform these stunts.

Why?

It is inadvisable to re-title some assets into the name of the trust. Deferred benefit assets, for example, are not re-titled. Such a re-titling of interest in a pension plan, IRA, profit sharing plan or 401K could cause an immediate, highly unfavorable income tax consequence; immediate income taxation plus imposition of a 10% surtax; if one is not old enough to be entitled to receive retirement benefits without penalty.

With deferred benefit assets, rather than re-titling the benefit, we tinker with the death beneficiary designation (more about that later). In similar vein, one normally does not transfer title to life insurance policies to the trust, but rather tinkers with the death beneficiary designations.

We will talk more about the integration of deferred benefit assets into a Living Trust Estate Plan in Chapter 8.

The Triangle

The points of the triangle represent the positions inherent in the living trust. These positions are:

The GRANTORS/SETTLORS: The people who cause the trust to be created and, usually, are the individuals who transfer their assets into the trust;

The TRUSTEES: After the titles to assets are transferred into the name of the trust, these are the people who control the assets now in the trust's name. They invest, borrow, lend, pledge as collateral and generally deal with the assets placed in the trust's name. Relying on our treasure chest metaphor; after the assets are placed in the trust the trustees carry the treasure chest down life's road. Periodically, the Trustees will reach into the treasure chest and distribute assets or income to an individual without expectation of any return thereof or therefor. The trust document limits the Trustees as to the objects of such largesse to:

The BENEFICIARIES: the people for whom the trust is created in the first place.

When these three positions are described to clients, they often conclude that, because there are three different positions in the trust, there must be three different people holding those positions. This is interpreted by many as a loss of control of assets to another. Something most of us loathe to do.

One nice thing about a Living Trust is that a single individual may legally occupy all three positions at once. The language creating the trust, thus, looks something like this:

Husband and Wife, as Grantors, contract with Husband and Wife, as Trustees, for the primary benefit of Husband and Wife, as Beneficiaries, to create the Husband and Wife Living Trust.

By virtue of holding all three positions inherent in the trust, the creators of the trust retain all powers incident to ownership of the underlying property. Obviously, this means that this trust, alone, will not prevent inclusion of all trust assets in the creator's taxable estate. However, let's defer the discussion of the estate tax savings aspects of trust usage to a later chapter. For now let's talk about the aspect of probate avoidance.

Probate Avoidance

Remember, whenever you see the word *probate*, the next word that should immediately spring to mind is the word *title*.

A trust is wonderfully adept at causing avoidance of the probate court system in the event of disability or death. Upon either event occurring to the Grantor of the trust (the former title holder of the property in the trust); the Grantor does not hold title to the asset. The trust is the title holder. Absent the creation of the trust and the transfer of title into the trust's name, title would be held in the Grantors name. Because the Grantor would be unable to sign his or her name in either event, title to assets would become "locked up." Absent the existence of the trust, action by the probate court to "unlock" title.

Additional terms in the trust concern replacement of trustees in the event of the Grantors disability or death. Thus, even though the Grantor of the trust becomes disabled or dies, the titles to the trust assets do not become "locked up". The trust provides for alternate, replacement trustees who are called upon and are empowered to serve as Trustees of the trust upon the death or disability of the Grantor/Trustee. Let's take an abbreviated look at some sample trust language:

In the event that either the Husband Grantor or the Wife Grantor becomes disabled while serving as a trustee, the other named Trustee shall continue to serve as sole Trustee, with full power, as trustee, to administer the trust and its assets for the primary mutual benefit of the Grantors.

In the event that both Grantors or the surviving Grantor becomes disabled or dies, then "Son #1"(or "Daughter #1" or whomever the grantors respectively choose) is appointed the first alternate successor trustee with full power to take control of the trust assets and administer same for the benefit of the Grantor(s) or the survivor of them.

The additional beauty of this trust language is that we can appoint as many sequentially serving successor trustees as we choose to name. Often, in larger estate, we recommend that the final alternate successor trustee named be a financial institution or its successor in interest to hedge the risk that all named successor trustees fail to survive the Grantor.

The important fact to note is that, by re-titling assets into the name of the trust <u>and</u> providing for an internal plan of successive trustees, the simple but important problem that causes probate in the first place is solved: the inability of the title owner to sign his signature, thereby causing the "lock down" of assets that only the order of the probate court can cure.

It should be obvious from the preceding discussion that, because successor trustees are appointed in the trust document, there is no need to resort to the probate court to "unlock assets" in the event of a Grantor's death. Even though a Grantor may die, there is still a trustee duly appointed and waiting to serve upon the Grantor's death because the trust language will provide some language like the following:

> Upon the death of the first Grantor to die; the other Grantor/ Trustee shall continue to serve as sole Trustee, with full power, as trustee, to administer the trust and its assets for the primary benefit of the surviving Grantor.

> Upon the death of the surviving Grantor, then "Son #1"(or "Daughter #1" or whomever the grantors respectively choose) is appointed the first alternate successor trustee with full power to take control of the trust assets and administer same for the benefit of the beneficiaries hereinafter identified.

As noted in the sample language, any number of alternate successor trustees can be designate to serve, either alone or with others as co-trustees, to continue the management of the trust's assets after the Grantor's death.

By virtue of the identification of alternate successor Trustees, the death of either or both of the Grantors does not result in the title holder of the asset's (the trust) inability to execute its signature. The combination of designation of any number of successor trustees and the final appointment of a commercial trust company (or the pronouncement of a methodology for appointment of additional successor trustees without the need for action by a court), assures that no court action will be required to "unlock the assets."

But how does a trust provide the direction that the Trustee will need (and usually provided by a Last Will and Testament in Probate) in order to manage the trust assets and distribute them according to the Grantor's wishes, after the Grantor's death?

Stated another way:

Upon the Grantor's death, to or for whom should the trustee distribute trust assets or continue to administer the trust and in what manner should the trustee accomplish these tasks?

For the answer to this question we must look to a different section of the trust document, the section that designates the successor beneficiaries of the trust. Again, to use some oversimplified language, such a trust section would look something like the following:

> Upon the death of the first Grantor to die, after satisfying all reasonable expenses arising out of the last illness and death of such Grantor (including estate and inheritance taxes due, if any) the Trustee shall continue to manage the trust assets for his or her primary benefit.
>
> Upon the death of the surviving Grantor, after satisfying all reasonable expenses arising out of the surviving Grantors last

illness and death (including estate and inheritance taxes, if any), the successor Trustee shall first allocate one share of the trust for each of Grantors' children then living and one share for each of Grantors' children who are then deceased, but who, in turn, are survived by descendants of their own, who shall share in the predeceased child's share in equal shares, per stirpes.

Per stirpes is a wonderful Latin term which estate planners like to bandy about. It makes them look really smart and it saves them a lot of time in writing. Per stirpes literally means "by representation".

By that term, an estate planner means that should someone in the line of distribution predecease any beneficiary in line before him and at the time of such death such deceased beneficiary is survived by descendants, then those descendants inherit the predeceased beneficiary's share proportionately, as determined by degree of relationship to the predeceased beneficiary. An example: may be in order:

Mom and Dad, the Grantors of a revocable living trust, have three sons, John, Joe and Jim. Each of these sons, in turn, has three children, Mom and Dad's grandchildren.

If Joe predeceases the survivor of Mom and Dad, Then Joe's children will receive what other wise would have been Joe's share, had he survived Mom and Dad; and those grandchildren of Mom and Dad will share Joe's share equally. Thus, at the latter death of Mom and Dad, John and Jim will each receive a one third share of the trust and the children of Joe will each receive one ninth (one third of Joe's one third share).

The foregoing trust language looks a lot like the language one might expect to see in a Last Will and Testament. There is a reason for that resemblance. Because substantially all of the Grantor's assets have been placed in the trust, at the time of death, the Grantor is the title owner of nothing. The trust holds title to all of the Grantor's assets. The beneficiary designation language substitutes for what would otherwise be "Will" language. It directs the successor trustee how to distribute the trust property outside the probate court process.

CONCLUSION:

Remember: The Probate Court does not make house calls.

If someone does not affirmatively place a problem before the court in the form of a petition in probate, the court does not go looking for problems to solve. The trust is the title owner of the assets. There is a designated successor trustee empowered to sign the trust's name and contractually obligated to perform the terms of the trust. The terms of the trust include the time and manner for distribution of the trust assets. Thus, there is mechanism for the transfer of title to assets without the need for probate court action. Even better, this mechanism is recognized as valid in all fifty states.

CHAPTER THREE

WHAT IS SO BAD ABOUT PROBATE ANYWAY?

Having just described how to successfully avoid probate court via the use of a revocable living trust, the next obvious question of the uninitiated is:

"What is so bad about Probate, anyway?"

How much time do you have?

It will take that long to adequately describe the misery that is the probate court. Regardless whether the procedure required is a conservatorship or a decedent estate, the disadvantages to probate court administration (in no particular order of emphasis) include:

- ♦ Unwanted Publicity;
- ♦ Loss of Control;
- ♦ Aggravation;
- ♦ Time Delay;
- ♦ Needless Expense.

Whether of a conservatorship or decedent estate, all of the records of the probate court are public. Not only does this mean that friends and neighbors can know your private financial business; but commercial services can look at a probate file and easily determine a person's assets and value, debts, identity of next of kin and beneficiaries and the amounts and timing of distributions to them. This leaves your family members open to, at the least, unwanted invasion of privacy by commercial vendors and, at the worst, bunko artists and con men at a time when they may be most emotionally vulnerable.

As to the other disadvantages of probate, let's look at each type of probate procedure and see exactly how these disadvantages are encountered. (For purposes of our illustrations, the following will describe the established probate procedures of the state of Missouri. While the state of Missouri has adopted the Uniform Probate Code, as have many other states, the exact procedure of a given probate court varies from state to state. To learn the specific probate procedure of your jurisdiction, resort should be had to a skilled estate planning attorney within your state.

Conservatorships:

The Procedure:

You will recall that conservatorships are probate

proceedings designed to unlock assets the titles of which have become locked up because of the disability of the title holder. Let me now describe the process in detail.

Appointment:

The conservatorship process commences with the filing of a Petition in the probate court. It suggests to the court that an individual has become disabled or incapacitated. It specifies, in laymen's terms, the nature and extent of the disability. The petition further states that the petitioner is able and willing to take over management of the disabled individual's assets and manage them according to law. It estimates the value of the property that will become subject to the probate court's jurisdiction if the conservatorship is created. It identifies by name and address the disabled person's nearest blood relatives and asks the court to appoint the petitioner conservator of the disabled person's estate.

Before filing this petition, the petitioner's attorney will send to the allegedly disabled person's attending physician a standardized questionnaire that asks about the nature and extent of the individual's alleged disability; the scope and course of the individual's immediate and long-term treatment; and the likelihood of continuation of the disability into the future. The physician completes and signs this form under oath. In the absence of any contested issues, the submission of this form will alleviate the need for the doctor's later appearance at court to testify as to the medical nature and extent of the alleged disability.

Upon receipt of this petition, the court appoints a nice young lawyer who needs work (and usually is of the same political affiliation as the probate judge) to act as the attorney ad litem for the allegedly disabled person. The job of this young lawyer is to meet the allegedly disabled person, his doctor and perhaps others close to the situation to determine the nature and extent of the individual's disability, in laymen's terms. It is this young attorney who represents the allegedly disabled individual, should an issue arise about whether the individual is so disabled as to be unable to manage his own affairs.

Notice is given to the immediate family that a petition has been filed which calls to question the ability of the individual to manage his own affairs; that the petitioner has volunteered to act as conservator; and that the recipient of the notice is invited to file any motions he desires in the matter and to attend the hearing which will be held (usually about 60-90 days down the road) to determine if the individual is disabled and to determine who should be appointed conservator of the individual's estate, should the court find the requisite disability to exist.

At the hearing the court will review the medical report; hear the report of the young lawyer regarding his/her personal observations concerning the nature and extent, if any, of the disabilities of the individual in question; and hear the testimony of all interested parties concerning the issues of disability, need for a conservatorship and propriety of appointment of the applicant as conservator. Usually the Petitioner is the only person to testify. He or she recites the day to day living style of the disabled person, placing particular emphasis upon the disabilities from which the individual suffers and how these disabilities negatively affect his/her ability to manage one's own financial affairs; and finally testifying that petitioner understands the legal obligations attendant to appointment as conservator and the individual's willingness and ability to undertake such obligations.

Upon conclusion of the testimony, the court awards a fee to the nice young attorney (around $400-$500). It sets a bond to secure the faithful performance of the conservator of his duties: usually in an amount equal to the value of the assets under administration (less the value of real estate which is not included in the amount of the bond). Once the bond is posted, the court grants to the conservator "Letters of Conservatorship". This document is tantamount to an operator's permit for the conservatorship. It is this document which entitles the conservator to "sign the name" of the disabled individual and thereby "unlock" his assets for his benefit.

What does this all cost?

Well, costs will vary from state to state; however, it will not be unreasonable to suggest the following figures: between $500-$750 for the petitioner's attorney; $400-$500 for that nice young ad litem attorney; filing fees of about $100; $150-$250 for the doctor's report; and an unknown amount for the bond premium, which varies in cost dependent upon the value of the underlying personal and mixed property.

Now; having obtained Letters of Conservatorship; can the Conservator now administer the disabled person's assets without further interference by the probate court?

You know better!

The Inventory:

The first task of the conservator is to prepare and make public by filing with the court an inventory which displays to the court and any member of the general public who chooses to come to the court house and look all of the disabled individual's assets that are under court supervision and their fair market value (as determined by appraisal) as of the date of commencement of the conservatorship. By the way, with increasing computerization of the probate courts records, it will soon be possible (if not already) to view these records from the comfort of one's home via internet access.

The Settlement(s):

After that, each year, on the anniversary date of the Conservator's appointment, the Conservator is obligated to present to the court a Settlement. This settlement must account to the court every penny which has come into the conservatorship during the just past year and account for every penny which has left the conservatorship during the just completed year. This accounting must be supported by back up documentation constituting a canceled check and an invoice or paid receipt.

The Audit(s):

The probate court staff will review each year's accounting for several requisites; mathematical accuracy, verification of expenditure; and legal compliance. It is this final aspect of the audit which causes the most aggravation in the management of conservatorships by the conservator.

When most people hear the term "legal compliance" they expect the term to mean " compliance with the law" in the investment and expenditure of conservatorship assets. So it does. However, when envisioning the terms of that compliance, most people believe that there is a statute, court rule, regulation or other published guideline for the conservator to follow and thereby

ensure that his management of the conservatorship is according to law. But guess what? In most states there are no such all encompassing laundry lists of do's and don'ts. Instead, it is left to the probate judge's discretion as to whether a given expenditure or investment is appropriate under the circumstances surrounding the individual disabled person's situation. While such adaptability may make sense in theory, in practice it can create a harrowing existence for the conservator.

Why?

Often probate judges informally adopt guidelines for investment and expenditure. The only problem with such a policy is that, more often than not, such guidelines are not published anywhere. Thus the Conservator must either rely on the expertise of the probate attorney he hires, to know the unwritten customs and mores of the particular probate judge or, before making any unusual or out of the ordinary expenditure, he must petition the court for permission to make the expenditure or investment. This, obviously, is the wiser course. for it is far better to know in advance that the court does not approve of a proposed expenditure or investment rather than after the particular transaction is made.

Why?

If the probate judge does not approve of the transaction and will not ratify it when asked to do so as part of the audit process, the conservator must reimburse the conservatorship estate from his/her private funds.

If the Conservator cannot replace the unapproved expenditure, the probate judge charges the bonding company. It then pays the amount back into the conservatorship and sues the conservator for breach of his/her fiduciary duties to the conservatorship.

What is the point of this explanation? Well there are several salient points to be made.

Loss of Control by Family:

First, and foremost, it is the probate judge, NOT the Conservator who is really in control of the funds entrusted to the conservatorship.

"So what?"

When the conservatorship is for your disabled spouse and the assets subject to the conservatorship are assets which you had always considered to be "family assets" over which you (along with your spouse) had complete control; the total loss of that control may seem inappropriate to you.

Aggravation:

Nevertheless the probate court makes no distinction between a spousal conservator and a child or for that matter a stranger. They are all bound by the same rules, policies and discretions of the probate judge. I think that it would be a bit redundant to elaborate at this point on the aspect of the aggravation implicit in such a conservatorship proceeding.

Cost:

Probate is costly. Because of the nature of the system, before any extraordinary expenditure is made, most smart conservators will petition the court for permission before actual investment or expenditure. In an average conservatorship that means that about two or three additional petitions will be filed each year to cover extraordinary situations.

As always, the cost of the process varies from state to state.

However, annual petitions for extraordinary expenses, coupled with the annual audit process, will usually result in attorneys fees (for a relatively modest sized conservatorship) in the range of several thousand dollars per year. This, just to keep the conservatorship operating properly.

How long will this process continue? Until one of

two events occurs; the disabled person regains the ability to manage his/her own financial affairs or dies.

By the way, attorneys and conservators are usually paid for their services in probate upon the basis of "reasonable compensation". This means that both the attorney and the conservator maintain time records which attest to their efforts in the operation of the conservatorship and the time it took to exert those efforts. Once a year, usually at the accounting period, these time records are submitted to the court for approval and award of fee. In the St. Louis metropolitan area "reasonable compensation" for the attorney is deemed to be $110.00 per hour and conservator's time is valued at a substantially lesser per hour sum.

Decedent Estates

The Procedure:

While the conservatorship procedure is fairly consistent throughout the country, decedent estate procedures vary greatly from state to state. Some states, like Colorado and New Jersey, are very user friendly, while others, like California, are highly supervised and expensive.

Many states follow the approach of the Uniform Probate Code. This is a model set of statutes developed by lawyers and legal educators which is meant to promote a standardized, consistent method of decedent estate administration. The Uniform code provides for two alternate types of decedent estate administration: supervised and unsupervised administration.

Appointment:

Both types of administration start with the filing of a petition that informs the court that some individual, a resident of the county within the court's jurisdiction, has died. The petition further informs the court of the age of the decedent and his/her last home address; Whether the decedent had a will, and if so, identifies the beneficiaries under the will and, despite the existence of a will, the identity of the beneficiaries as defined by state law when there are no Last Will and Testament. It further requests the court to appoint the applicant Personal Representative, to administer the decedent estate according to law and after that make distribution of the assets of the estate according to either the Will or the intestacy code, as appropriate.

The Inventory:

Upon the grant of Letters Testamentary, in the event that a Will exists, or Letter of Administration, in the event that there is no Will, the legatees and heirs at law are notified of the issuance of the letters. This is the notice to heirs that administration of the deceased's affairs is about to commence.

Thereafter, within thirty days of appointment, the Personal Representative is required to file an inventory of the estate, displaying the identity and date of death value of the assets of which the deceased died sole or in common title holder at the time of his death. As in Conservatorships, this inventory and all other documents are available for public inspection.

In many states inheritance tax assessors are then appointed to assess state tax obligations, although, increasingly states are opting to assess an estate tax in lieu of inheritance tax; because the labor of reviewing the return and contesting value then lays primarily with the IRS rather than a state department of revenue.

The Claim Period:

Most states' decedent estate procedures allow for what is known as a claim period. This is the period of time during which creditors of a deceased person have their final chance to receive payment from the deceased person's estate. Most states' laws provide that if a creditor of the deceased person does not file its claim during the claim period, absent having a security interest in a specific asset, it is forever barred from seeking repayment from the deceased person's assets. Most states' statutes provide for a claim period of six months' duration.

Most states' statutes also provide that the limitation period on claims does not apply to state or federal taxing authorities.

The Settlement(s):

Supervised Administration:

Where the administration is supervised, it operates much like conservatorship administration. All expenditures and investments during the estate's administration are subject to the court's supervisory review and the same risks and loss of family control prevail.

Unsupervised Administration:

In an unsupervised administration, however, after the filing of the inventory, the personal representative has some measure of autonomy in the administration of the decedent estate. Unless someone complains to the court that the personal representative is acting improperly or is failing to act, the court will not interfere, or even look at, for that matter, the personal representative's administration of the decedent estate.

Distribution Procedure:

Supervised Administration

After all of the appropriate tasks of administration have been performed, the executor is ready to close the estate and make distribution to the persons entitled (either under the will or according to law) to distribution. This distribution is made by re-titling the estate's assets into the name of the appropriate beneficiary of the estate.

In order to accomplish this, the executor must first publish and mail a Notice to the proposed beneficiaries that a Final Settlement will be filed upon a certain date and advising such beneficiaries to come forward and make any complaints which they may have regarding the estate administration. Upon the appointed day the executor files a final settlement which is audited.

After the audit process is complete, (including the approval of any Petitions for Ratification of Expenditures which the audit staff required as a precondition to audit approval) the court will review the Petition for Final Distribution which the executor filed at the same time as the Final Settlement.

This Petition informs the court, in summary fashion, what has transpired during the administration process; that the estate is now in a condition such that closing of the estate is proper; and the identity of the proposed distributees, as well as the proposed distribution of the estate's assets to such distributees.

Assuming that the probate judge finds that all matters are in proper order, he will enter an Order of Final Distribution. This order directs the executor to make the distribution of estate assets and instructs the executor as to which assets are to be distributed to which beneficiaries so as to properly conform to the dictates of the Will or the Statute for distribution, when there is no Will.

Upon such distribution, the executor is required to obtain receipts from each beneficiary which acknowledge that such beneficiary has received distribution of the assets which constitute such beneficiary's share of the estate. When the executor files these receipts with the court, to prove that proper distribution of estate assets has been complete; the probate administration ends.

Unsupervised Administration

At the conclusion of an unsupervised administration, the personal representative (executor) files a Statement of Account in lieu of a Settlement. The Statement of Account is not audited as is a Settlement. Instead of a Petition for Final Distribution of the estate, the personal representative files a Schedule of Distribution that describes to the court the assets remaining for distribution after payment of all lawful expenses and lists the persons to whom distribution is proposed to be made and in what proportion or amount.

The court does not review these documents filed in an independent administration, as it does the documents filed in an audited supervised administration. Instead, a notice is sent to the proposed heirs and distributees informing them that the schedule and statement have been filed with the court; that for a period of time (usually 20-30 days) the documents may be reviewed after which, if no objection is made thereto, distribution is made by the personal representative, without further review or order of the court.

The Personal Representative is still required to obtain receipts to prove that proper distribution has been made. Upon the filing of such receipts with the court, the independent administration ends.

Although an unsupervised administration allows the personal representative a substantially greater amount of control during administration; both types of decedent estate administration should be avoided whenever possible because, whether supervised or unsupervised, the costs of administration can be identical and substantial.

The Curse of Service Fees in Decedent Estates

The largest source of complaint from decedent estate clients is the service fees engendered by the probate process; the attorneys fees and personal representative or executor fees. The manner of computation of these fees varies from state to state. I have included an appendix which lists the methods of computation of decedent estate fees so that you can see your state's provisions therefor. Although there is variation in the methods, they distill down to two basic computations.

Reasonable Compensation

Reasonable compensation is the standard set in many states and it is left to the individual trial judge of the given jurisdiction to decide what is reasonable per hour rates for his jurisdiction. Where reasonable compensation is the established system, the court reviews the tasks undertaken, the time spent per task and assesses an hourly rate of compensation for the services valuable to the administration of the estate.

Statutory Minimum fees:

However, in many states in lieu of, or besides, reasonable compensation, there is provided compensation in the form of a "minimum fee schedule". This is usually a sliding scale percentage of the asset value (or some part of it) under administration. For example, in Missouri, both the personal representative and the attorney for the estate are entitled to a minimum fee computed as follows:

The following percentages apply to the value of the personal property administered and the proceeds of all real property sold under order of the probate court:

On the first	$ 5,000	5%
On the next	$20,000	4%
On the next	$75,000	3%
On the next	$300,000	2-3/4%
On the next	$600,000	2-1/2%
On all over	$1,000,000	2%

According to a national survey, when the personal representative and attorney's fees are combined, on estates of a value of more than $100,000, the national average percentage loss of estate value to service fees in probate is 7-1/2% of the gross value, as defined above. While 7-1/2% may not seem like a lot to some, most people are surprised at how large the actual number value is when seen in print. To give you an idea of the types of numbers I am talking about, see the chart which appears on the following page:

National Average Fee Assessments

Gross Estate Size	Probate Fees
$ 100,000	$ 7,500
$ 200,000	$ 15,000
$ 300,000	$ 22,500
$ 400,000	$ 30,000
$ 500,000	$ 37,500

$ 600,000	$ 45,000
$ 700,000	$ 52,500
$ 800,000	$ 60,000
$ 900,000	$ 67,500
$1,000,000	$ 75,000
$1,500,000	$112,500
$2,000,000	$150,000
$2,500,000	$187,500
$3,000,000	$225,000

Remember, these percentages are applied against the gross value of assets; whereas beneficiaries inherit the net value, after payment of claims and expenses, including attorney and executors fees.

Thus, for many, the sad realization is that, along with your children and other intended beneficiaries there are substantial unintended beneficiaries, the service providers in probate; often the single largest beneficiaries of the estate!

Remember, too, that the only person with authority to "unlock" the title to real estate in case of title holder's death is the probate judge of the county in which the property is located. This means that, although you can only die once, you can have multiple probates and be susceptible to multiple probate fee assessments.

The statutory fee schedule causes inclusion of unanticipated beneficiaries to your estate:

The statutory fee schedule causes inclusion of unanticipated beneficiaries to your estate:

Your Executor and Your Attorney.

What's worse; they may inherit more of your estate than your intended beneficiaries.

In today's society, this is not very unusual. Perhaps you have a vacation condominium in a southeastern state. A condominium is an interest in real estate and requires a separate probate. How about that timeshare on Hilton Head Island where you vacation one week each year? Under South Carolina law, timeshare interests are considered real property. Upon a title holder's death there will need to be a probate in South Carolina as well as in the county of the individual's residence.

CONCLUSION:

Whether in the form of a Conservatorship or a Decedent Estate Administration; Probate Court Processes generate publicity at times when most individuals desire privacy; can subject your family to unwanted commercial solicitation, or worse, bunko schemes which take advantage of the unwary at times when they are most vulnerable; possible loss of control of assets during the administration process;

time delay of distribution of assets due to the inherent probate process; and substantial, needless expense.

CHAPTER FOUR

THE MOST COMMON PLANNING OPTIONS

Let's look at the implications of how joint tenancy actually operates. In each instance, the implication is negative in nature and constitutes real liabilities to using joint tenancy as your primary estate planning vehicle!

Loss of Control

Often, when planning for wealthy clients, I can save them literally hundreds of thousands of estate tax dollars through sophisticated estate planning techniques (which are, frankly, outside the purview of this book). Despite the potential savings, many clients refuse to draft the plan. Why? Inherent in the plan is some loss of control of the assets utilized in the particular technique. (Remember those incidences of ownership, previously discussed?)

Yet those same individuals will think nothing of putting their children's names, as joint tenants, on the titles to their assets, not realizing that in so doing, they have given up all control of their assets! How can this be? Well, remember, for the bulk of one's assets, when you place another individual on the title to an asset as joint tenant, thereafter, to do anything with the asset, the joint title holder must sign the title document! This, necessarily, means that the joint title holder now has veto power over the real owner.

When I suggest this to many of my clients their reply is along the following line:

> I am not worried about that. I raised my kids right! They'll do whatever I tell them to do!

I long ago learned that if I were to retain clients, it was not in my best interest to question their parenting skills.

So, instead, I pose the following question:

> How well did you raise your sons and daughters-in-law?

Because if your children are married, you'll need their spouse's permission, as well.

Nearly all states have statutes which provide for some type of marital rights for a surviving spouse in the property of the other spouse. This so even if held in the other's sole name, should the other spouse die first. Sometimes these rights are called "Dower" and "Curtesy" rights. In some states these states are called spousal statutory rights. Whatever the name, the effect of these statutes is the same. A surviving spouse has a property interest in the property of a deceased spouse.

For a spouse to convey away separately titled property without receiving adequate consideration therefor is said to be in fraud of his spouse's rights. It is deemed a "fraudulent conveyance" which can be later challenged by the surviving spouse when discovered. To prevent surviving spouses from wreaking havoc in the marketplace by claiming that their predeceased spouse transferred assets without the survivor's knowledge and for less than fair value; all commercial markets require the signature of both spouses, to transfer title to an asset; even though the name of one spouse does not appear on the record title.

Thus, when you include your children as joint title holders of your assets, you'd best remain on good terms with your in-laws . . . all of them. If your child's mate refuses to sign the title document, you can do nothing with your own asset.

Increased Risk of Conservatorship

Another result of the true nature of joint tenancy is that for each additional joint tenant you add to the title, you are increasing the risk that the asset in question will be subjected to a conservatorship.

Remember, when you add a name to the title to an asset as joint tenant, while you may think that what you are doing is providing a future inheritance right, the actuality is that you are conveying a present title interest in and to the asset to the just named joint tenant.

What happens if the newly named joint tenant (or his/her spouse) becomes disabled?

If any joint tenant cannot sign the title document, the asset becomes "locked up" and the proposed transaction cannot be completed. How do we "unlock" the asset's title? C'mon, you remember! We go to the probate court and create a conservatorship so that a court appointed conservator (with the court's permission) can sign the title document. After the asset is sold, what happens to the sale proceeds? Well maybe the judge will agree with your position that in creating the joint tenancy you only intended to create a future right of inheritance.

On the other hand, maybe he will read the law literally and decide that, notwithstanding your testimony, your real intention was to provide your now disabled child a present interest in the asset at the time you put his name on the title. If the judge takes the latter course, you can expect that, before you leave the probate court, you will leave that now disabled child's proportionate share of the asset's sale proceeds in the conservatorship.

Increased Risk of Loss of the Asset

There is another risk encountered when you place your child's name on the title to your assets . . . the increased risk of loss of the asset itself!

Here is the scenario. Let's say that you have just placed your child's name on the title to all of your assets and to celebrate this exercise of largesse, you plan a little celebration at your favorite restaurant and, naturally, invite your child. He takes off work early in order to properly prepare for this momentous occasion. In his hurry, he runs a yellow/red traffic light and collides with a school bus thereby creating 25 quadriplegic children. There is no amount of liability insurance that will cover this loss. After the plaintiffs' attorneys obtain the policy limits, they start looking for other assets against which they can levy to provide for their clients' acute personal needs.

Do you really think that when those attorneys come knocking upon your door to seize your assets (of which your son is a joint title owner) those attorneys are going to walk away empty handed after you explain that your intent in placing your son's name on the title was only to create a right of inheritance in the future? Guess again!

Ineffective Disability Plan

Besides the rationale of inexpensive inheritance planning, the other reason people recite for placing others' names in joint tenancy on their assets is to provide for an inexpensive disability plan. This rationale is stated as follows:

Well, I want to put my nephew, Timmy, on the title because he is the relative who lives closest to me. If anything happens to me, he can get at my assets and use them to pay my bills and take care of me.

What's wrong with this rationale?

It won't work! Once the bank accounts and CDs are expended, all other assets will not be available to Timmy. Once outside the ambit of the limited "special Statutes" class of assets, it takes the signature of all title holders (and their spouses) to do anything with the asset.

Repeat after me:

Joint Tenancy designation as a tool for disability planning simply does not work!

So, let's review!

The good news about joint tenancy is that if everybody dies in the right order, the anticipated plan of inheritance will work.

The bad news about joint tenancy is that if anybody dies in an unanticipated order, not only will the plan not work, it will probably disinherit an intended beneficiary. In its creation you have surrendered control over your own assets, not only to the intended beneficiary but to his/her spouse, as well. You have increased the risk that the asset will become part of a conservatorship because of disability of a title holder and, in so becoming, you will lose the proportionate value of the asset immediately. You have increased the risk of loss as a result of someone else's negligence, wrongdoing or breach of contract; and as an inexpensive disability protection plan, it just doesn't work.

It just seems to me that when you stack up the pros and cons, only a fool would hold assets in joint tenancy as a means of insuring a scheme of inheritance.

NONPROBATE TRANSFER TITLES:
The TODs and PODs

After discussing the evils of joint tenancy in my seminar, the next question then asked is :

What about T.O.D. and P.O.D. designations?

T.O.D stands for "Transfer on Death". P.O.D. stands for "Pay on Death".

Many states have created statutes which allow re-titling of assets using one or the other of these terms and then the listing of one or more intended beneficiaries who, by virtue of the designation become the title owner of the asset immediately upon the death of the main titleholder. No additional action of any type is required in order to vest title in the beneficiary. This means that there is no requirement of probate upon the primary titleholder's death.

States which have enacted such statutes have done so in order to protect people who wished to avoid probate and the negative aspects of joint tenancy from incompetent drafting by attorneys.

At common law, a solution to the negative control and risk of loss aspects of joint tenancy could be obtained by holding title to assets in what was known as a defeasible life estate. This meant that the titleholder changed the title so that, instead of holding title as absolute owner of the asset, the titleholder head the asset for his life, only, subject to the right to own the asset thereafter by certain designated beneficiary. However, the titleholder reserved to himself the power to sell or otherwise deal with the asset. This meant that the title holder could sell, lease, mortgage, barter, and generally engage in any commercial transaction with regards to the property during his life and the remainder beneficiaries only received absolute title to what remained at the time of the titleholder's death.

While this was a valuable title designation vehicle, the biggest drawback to it is that it is very difficult to properly draft the title designation.. In Missouri the state bar probate and trust law committee, having seen so many titles butchered virtually beyond repair by improper drafting, decided to protect the public from such tortured drafting by statutorily creating a simple designation which would create the same effect as the complex common law designation.

Advantages over Joint Tenancy

The greatest advantage of this type of title designation over joint tenancy is that, where available, the T.O.D. designee has no ownership interest in the underlying property until the moment of the titleholder's death. This, then successfully resolves the problems of loss of control and expansion of risk of conservatorship and loss through liability of joint tenants. As between the two, T.O.D. designations are clearly superior to joint tenancy as a probate avoidance technique.

Remaining Disadvantages

There are substantial disadvantages to the use of such designations, however.

The biggest disadvantage is the inability to perform comprehensive, contingent distribution planning. While it is true that where statutes exist which allow such contingent titling (the statute usually provides that the title owner can revoke or amend the designation at any time during life and can utilize the underlying asset in any manner without the need for consent of the contingent distributee) some, extremely limited contingent planning can occur, (i.e.):

Upon my death to my children in equal shares, per stirpes.

None of the statutes require any third party to accept a T.O.D. designation. The result of this is that banks and brokerages and the like will not allow any designation, the interpretation of which is questionable or requiring more than a sixth grade education for interpretation.

Why ?

Because the banks and brokerages do not want to incur the risk of improperly interpreting the designation.

Thus, I know of no financial institution which will accept other than the most simple designation. The example above is about as complex as one can make a designation and have any reasonable expectation of acceptance by a financial institution.

This means, of course, that there can be not complex contingent plan of distribution. Likewise there can be no complex schedule of distribution for underage beneficiaries. If a minor is designated and the titleholder dies, for example, there will have to be created a conservatorship to hold title for the minor child. Then, even worse, to most people's thinking, the minor will receive complete distribution at age eighteen, as we have already discussed.

Last Will and Testament Planning

What is a Will?

It depends upon the state of your domicile's laws.

However, in general, a Will can be defined as follows:

a writing, signed by an individual and witnessed by at least two (in some states three) individuals who have or will receive no interest in the writer's assets as a result of his death; which designates to whom his assets will pass as a result of his death and designates the individual who has the authority to cause the transfers to occur.

There is absolutely nothing wrong with using a Will as your primary estate planning vehicle.

But it is important to understand both what a will does and does not do.

The Two Most Common Misperceptions About Wills

♦ They are effective while the Maker is alive.

♦ They create probate avoidance upon death.

A skilled professional can provide comprehensive, contingent inheritance planning in the body of a Will, as well as substantially beneficial estate tax planning. Just keep in mind the purpose of a Will and its attendant costs.

Many times people mistake Wills for Durable Powers of Attorney. I have often received phone calls which inquire why no one will follow the individual's directions or give the individual access to a disabled relative's assets even after the individual has shown the third party (the banker, broker etc.) the disabled person's will, which clearly identifies the individual as the disabled person's personal representative.

The answer lies in the fact that, due to its legal nature, the personal representative appointed in a person's Last Will and Testament receives no power to act until two things occur. The testator (writer of the will) dies and the will is admitted to probate and letters testamentary are granted to the named personal representative. It is only within the context of a probate proceeding in the probate court that a personal representative is empowered.

Unfortunately, where this mistake is made, it is usually the case that by the time the "personal representative" learns that he/she has no power, the disabled testator no longer has sufficient mental or physical capacity to execute a durable power of attorney, which would allow the designated attorney-in-fact, to manage the disabled person's financial affairs. At such point, the only way to take control of the disabled individual's finances is through the establishment of a conservatorship in probate.

Because a Will only takes affect at death, if a Will is to be the primary estate planning document, a Durable Power of Attorney is an essential document to the overall estate plan. The Power of Attorney will provide the necessary authority to an appropriately named individual to take control of a disabled Testator's (Will writer's) assets, without the need for intervention of the probate court.

One of the other most common misconception concerning wills is that, somehow, a Will causes probate avoidance. I can't count the number of times clients have entered my office and started our conference by saying:

I want you to write me a Will so that, when I die, my assets won't have to probated. My uncle's estate went through probate and it was nothing but aggravation and expense. Write a Will so my heirs won't have to endure that.

My standard reply to such a request is as follows:

Wills do not avoid probate. They anticipate probate. A Will is nothing more than a road map for the probate judge to in the course of the administration of your probate estate; telling him how to administer the estate and to whom to make distribution upon its end.

I will not repeat my previous sermon regarding the costs and other disadvantages of a decedent estate probate administration. suffice to say, I believe that the cost, aggravation, publicity, possible loss of control of assets during the process mitigate against utilizing the probate court for family wealth transfers. However, if you want the supposed security that a probate process provides some individuals, then, by all means utilize a will as you primary estate planning vehicle.

Just Remember:

When you execute your will you are making your advanced reservation for your assets to go through Probate Court at the time of your death

Planning Utilizing Living Trusts:

Without repeating the recitation of virtues of Revocable Living Trusts; let's, at least briefly compare them to the other just described planning vehicles.

A Trust is the only single planning vehicle available which will protect you from the costs of probate in the event of your disability and/or death and still allow you to retain full and complete control of your assets an planning without interference by anyone.

While you can write a durable power of attorney and re-title assets in joint tenancy or with T.O.D. designations; you will not thereby be able to establish a comprehensive plan for distribution of your assets, regardless of the circumstances existing at the time of your death; and you will not be able to time delay the enjoyment of distribution by beneficiaries who are too young or otherwise disabled. Moreover, it is practically impossible to avoid possible severe adverse estate tax consequences utilizing these titleholder designations.

While you can write a will and a durable power of attorney, and thereby provide for complex contingent designation of beneficiaries and distribution of benefit and perform wondrous estate tax planning; the will itself anticipates that there shall be a probate administration at the time of your death along with the accompanying fees, costs and other disadvantageous aspects.

It is only through the use of a Revocable Living Trust that you can obtain all of one's usual planning goals and avoid the unnecessary cost and expense of probate systems.

Remember, as much as it provides cost efficiency, a Revocable Living Trust provides something else of far greater benefit; the true reason for engaging in estate planning; peace of mind.

It is only through the use of a Revocable Living Trust that you can be certain that the assets which you have worked your whole life to acquire and maintain will, in the vent of your disability be administered by the individuals or entities of your choosing, as you desire to take care of yourself and those you love, during that disability, and, thereafter, cause your assets to be managed and distributed by the people you trust, to the people you desire to benefit, at the time and in the manner which you desire, at the least cost possible, avoiding, conservatorship and decedent estate costs, minimizing estate taxation; accomplishing all of the above no matter what the circumstances, at the time of your death.

CONCLUSION:

While each common planning techniques available, in certain circumstances, provides some sort of benefit; only a Living Trust can provide seamless, comprehensive estate planning which will protect you from Conservatorships, in the event of your disability; Decedent Estates, upon your death; allow you full control of designation of your asset managers, (and the terms subject to which they will manage) to manage your assets for your and your family's benefit at times when you cannot; provide an enforceable, comprehensive plan of distribution; and accomplish all of these benefits at the least possible cost.

CHAPTER FIVE

ESTATE TAXATION THE BASICS

Earlier in this book we discussed what constituted an estate for estate tax planning purposes. Now it is time to try to explain how the value previously determined is taxed under the U.S. Estate Tax Code.

In previous editions of this book, I spent extensive time and pages discussing the Estate Tax Code. How it affected middle class families. How best to legally avoid its draconian decimation of family wealth from generation to generation.

However, as a result of the most recent revision of the tax code (effective January 1, 2013) most middle class families will not experience those former disastrous effects.

Because of these changes in the law, this chapter will discuss the present condition of the law. Chapters in previous editions of this book that extensively discussed estate tax savings techniques I have now relegated to the appendix of this book. I have done this so that in the event that in the future Congress determines to use the estate tax code as a revenue raiser, you can refer to the Appendix to see some of the techniques that estate planning attorneys have traditionally utilized to protect family wealth.

(Remember, on average, Congress has tinkered with the estate tax code every several years and there is no reason to suspect that this legislative habit is about to change.)

So, just a few facts about estate tax law as it presently exists:

As a result of the most recent tax law change, an individual's estate must exceed $5,250,000 before he or she will experience an estate tax consequence.

The discussion in the appendix as to how the law operates (unified credits and the like) is still applicable. It is just that the unified credit is now $2,045,800.

And even better, that amount is indexed for inflation.

There is one new substantial change in the law that directly affects married couples positively. That change is called "portability".

Under prior law, throughout its long history, the law provided that if one's estate was not sufficiently large to utilize one's full estate tax credit, the unused portion was forfeited.

However, the new law provides that for a married couple, the unused portion of the estate tax credit of the first spouse to die can be transferred to the surviving spouse's taxable estate. Thus the unused portion of the credit is "portable"

The import of this for a married couple is that, even without "sophisticated" estate tax planning a married couple can shelter from estate taxation up to $10,500,000.

As is always the case with the federal tax code, however, there is an important trick one must employ in order to obtain this tax benefit.

The law has always provided that if one's gross estate did not exceed the "asset equivalent value" of the estate tax credit (in 2013, $ 5,250,000) there is no obligation to file an estate tax return.

However, this new tax law provides that in order for the surviving spouse to "inherit" the unused tax credit of his/her predeceased spouse, the surviving spouse must elect to do so at the time of the first spouse's death, by making an election to do so on the predeceased spouse's duly filed estate tax return.

Thus, even if there is no obligation to file an estate tax return at the time of the first spouse to die's death, in order to claim the unused tax credit, the surviving spouse must make sure that an estate tax return is filed to secure the benefit.

Notwithstanding this great change in the law, many estate planning attorney's believe that it is wise to engage in traditional estate tax planning for married couples.

The reason; what the government giveth, the government can taketh away.

Many knowledgeable estate planning attorneys believe that the concern over budgetary deficits will cause Congress to return the exclusion and its corresponding asset equivalent value to a much lower number in the near future. Moreover, in the entire history of the estate tax code, there has never been a concept like "portability" of a person's unused estate tax credit until just this year.

For this reason, while I have moved the discussion of the basic operation of the estate tax system and the Chapters on sophisticated estate tax avoidance strategies to the appendix of this book, I have also moved to the appendix my discussion of the most common estate tax planning strategy for married couples. This strategy is essential to protect married couples, should Congress revoke "Portability" and reduce the estate tax credit to a more modest number.

Two more points:

If by some miracle you are subject to estate tax under existing law, the effective tax rate is 40%.

The gift tax laws are still in effect. (most people don't such laws exist).

For the uninitiated, if you make a gift to another person of substantial value (I leave it to you to define that term) there is a transfer tax payable by the giver of the gift, not the recipient, of 40% of the value of the gift. The good news is that there is a tax exemption on the amount of gifts made to any one person per year of $14,000. As you will see in the appendix chapter on sophisticated tax techniques, this annual exclusion is a key component in many of these strategies.

On final note about gift taxation. That unified estate tax credit is also available to protect otherwise taxable gifts. In other words, if you gave $25,000 to a child, the first $14,000 would be protected by the annual gift exclusion this year. If you so chose, rather than pay the tax on the excess value, you could, instead, file a gift tax return and apply part of your estate tax credit to the tax generated but the excess gift. The end result, the entire gift escapes taxation but the amount sheltered by the unified estate tax credit at death is reduced by the amount of tax sheltered in the year of the gift.

Finally, Missouri has no estate tax or gift tax at the present time, while other states have estate and gift tax codes independent of federal law.

CONCLUSION:

Because of recent federal tax law changes, estate taxation no longer affects the vast majority of middle class members as it once did.

Even if you are not subject to federal estate tax, depending upon your state of residence, you may be subject to state estate or inheritance tax and, depending on the state, the tax can be quite substantial.

Accordingly, when planning one's estate, it is always wise to check with an estate planning attorney to determine the present condition of the law on both the federal and state levels (it seems to continually change) and to determine, notwithstanding the presently generous provisions of the law, whether some sort of estate tax planning is advisable, given your specific circumstances.

CHAPTER SIX

RETIREMENT BENEFITS: ARE BENEFICIARY DESIGNATIONS ENOUGH?

For many people retirement benefits (IRAs, 401Ks, 403Bs and deferred stock benefits while there are substantial differences, for our simplistic discussion we are going to refer to all of them here as IRAs) constitute the single largest component of their estate.

It is not unusual today to see a typical client who has an estate consisting of a home worth $250,000, bank and brokerage accounts worth $50-60,000, life insurance with a death benefit value of $50,000 two cars and a retirement plan benefit exceeding $300,000.

It always amazes me when advising clients,

that many are (rightly) concerned with developing a complex, contingent plan for the transfer of their "non-qualified" (read, "non-IRA") assets but are quite unconcerned about their retirement benefits.

Why?

The answer is because they think that by virtue of the beneficiary designation that their employer or the bank required them to fill out when establishing the retirement account, that they have adequately integrated that asset into their estate plan.

One of the tests to use to determine whether your attorney is a skilled estate planning attorney (more on that in the later chapters) is to see what he suggests regarding the structuring of those retirement plan benefits in your overall estate plan.

Quite frankly if your attorney believes that a simple death beneficiary designation is an adequate planning tool for those retirement benefits, maybe this is not the estate planning "expert" for you.

The sad fact of the matter is that the simple designation of your spouse as primary beneficiary and your children as contingent beneficiaries is a totally inadequate beneficiary designation.

Why?

- ♦ Ask yourself the following questions, some of which you may never have considered:

- ♦ What happens if, at the time of my death, my designated beneficiary is substantially disabled?

- ♦ What happens if, at the time of my death, one of my designated beneficiaries is a minor?

- ♦ What happens if, at the time of my death, one of my designated beneficiaries is less than responsible?

If any of these situations were to exist, not only would you plan not work, but it might cause more harm than good.

Why?

Because, a beneficiary of an IRA is required to make certain elections as to how he wants the benefit paid out in order to avoid near immediate income taxation of the inherited IRA benefit.

I'll get to the IRA distribution options in just a minute. But first let's cover some basic problems that can arise as a result of the need to make elections to avoid the worst income tax consequences possible.

If the beneficiary is substantially disabled or is a minor (which, as we have previously discussed is a disability in and of itself) the beneficiary literally cannot make the elections!

In order to empower someone to make the elections most beneficial to the beneficiary someone has to be legally appointed to make them.

Think hard now, who might that be?

Of course, absent advanced planning (in this case for the IRA beneficiary) a conservator has to be appointed to make the necessary tax elections. And I am sure you remember the nightmare of conservatorships I have previously described.

But what's worse, let's presume that the beneficiary is either a minor or falls into that category of financially irresponsible.

Now the problem becomes how to protect such a beneficiary from himself. While the usual concern is how to ensure that the tax benefit is obtained, in the latter two examples (a minor or irresponsible beneficiary) the problem is more basic.

How do we protect the beneficiary from

choosing to take a lump sum distribution?

As previously discussed, most clients with young children are primarily concerned with protecting their children from their own poor decision making born out of the inexperience of youth.

Simply stated, by simply filling in the blank on the death beneficiary designation form, it is impossible to protect a beneficiary from himself. Once the child turn 18, he has the right to control the distribution of the IRA, just as an irresponsible adult (regardless of age) can so do.

Past experience shows that the all too common occurrence with such beneficiaries is that they elect a lump sum distribution. The disastrous results are twofold.

Income tax deferral is lost.

The beneficiary has unrestricted control over what is often the largest part of his inheritance, with usually disastrous results then occurring.

So, if you wish to protect a spouse, child or grandchild from himself and wish to do so in a manner that is efficient as to cost, aggravation and maintaining control in people of your choosing, the best course of action is to designate a properly drafted trust as the IRA beneficiary.

Now let's go back to that "test your attorney's estate planning expertise" issue.

For many years the only person, other than the IRA owner, who could defer income taxation of the death benefit beyond the year after the owner's death was the owner's spouse. Everyone else could only take a lump sum distribution.

A lump sum distribution meant the end of the IRA and immediate income taxation of the entire death benefit.

Because of this, attorneys would always advise an estate planning to client to designate his spouse as the primary beneficiary and his trust as the death beneficiary. In that way the spouse could rollover the IRA and continue income tax deferral. Since the tax deferral ended for everyone else, by designating the trust as the contingent beneficiary, the net proceeds of the IRA became subject to the complex, contingent distribution plan contained in the trust. In such manner the need for a conservatorship was avoided and minor or financially irresponsible beneficiaries were protected from themselves.

However, about a decade ago, Congress changed the income tax laws regarding IRA distributions, and these changes greatly benefit the death beneficiaries of an IRA.

While a non-spouse beneficiary cannot "rollover" the IRA, he can "stretch" the IRA.

This means the death beneficiary no longer has to "cash out" the IRA and pay taxes immediately.

Instead, a non-spouse beneficiary has choices as to how he takes distributions from the IRA.

Depending on the circumstances, he can:

- ♦ Take a lump sum distribution and pay all of the taxes right away;

- ♦ Take a 5 year payout;

- ♦ Stretch the payout over the remaining amortizable life of the deceased IRA owner;

Or

- ♦ Stretch the payout over his own mortality life;

(Think of this amortizable life business much

like an annuity payment each year for the remainder of the beneficiary's life, the length of which is determined according to IRS tables.)

Not all of these options are available to every death beneficiary. Factors such as whether the IRA owner was already taking required distributions when he died; whether the beneficiary was expressly designated or became a beneficiary according to the terms of the IRA in absence of a designated beneficiary can alter the options available.

The point to be made is that, whereas in the past, sound legal advice as to what to do with an IRA was a no-brainer for an attorney; now it takes a knowledgeable estate planning attorney to help structure a plan of distribution for IRAs, just as in the case for all one's other assets. The knee-jerk answer will only maximize both the tax loss and the risk of loss of principal.

So, if in seeking the advice of an attorney you disclose that you have "substantial" retirement benefits and he doesn't discuss how to integrate those benefits into your estate plan so as to provide the same detailed provisions you have devised to protect your beneficiaries from the government and themselves, that is not the attorney you want to help you plan your estate.

So what should he suggest?

As always, the specific plan details depend on your specific family situations and your personal concerns. However, use of an IRA trust is the most efficient and effective method available to minimize adverse income tax consequences and risk of loss of the value of inheritance.

However, by designating a separate Retirement Benefit Protection Trust as the death beneficiary of your IRA you can ensure that the person of your choosing makes the IRS required elections in timely manner to insure that the least amount of income taxes possible reduce your beneficiaries' inheritance. Such a trust can also protect a beneficiary from his own financial inexperience or weakness, while still providing a mechanism for access to the benefit beyond the "minimum" should the need arise.

Additionally, if a beneficiary is or becomes disabled in the future, by designating a properly drafted protection trust as the beneficiary you may be able protect the retirement benefit from needless spend down otherwise required in order to obtain Medicaid subsidation.

Why a Separate Trust?

Because of the complex IRS restrictions on IRA distributions, if we just designated your revocable trust as the death beneficiary of the IRA (the old knee-jerk advice) the odds are that maximum income tax savings would be lost.

As is often the case when dealing with the IRS, you have to jump through more than a few hoops to obtain the maximum tax benefit available.

While it is possible to draft two totally separate distribution provisions in your trust; one for IRA benefits and one for everything else, I have found that clients, successor trustees and beneficiaries (not to mention the IRS) become really confused when trying to interpret two separate distribution provisions than operate at the same time. The last thing one wants when dealing with distributions and taxes is confusion on anyone's part. Thus I find that most clients prefer to separate distribution of IRA benefits from everything else.

Conclusion:

A simple "form" IRA beneficiary designation will not adequately protect your intended beneficiaries from themselves of the government.

Because of the complex IRS regulations governing the deferral of income tax consequences of distribution choices available, it takes a trusted, knowledgeable advisor to help you structure the inheritance of IRA benefits.

The best way to structure the inheritance of IRA benefits is through the use of a special trust specifically drafted to ensure that your intended beneficiaries are protected from needless income taxation and their own weaknesses.

CHAPTER SEVEN

PLANNING FOR THE DISABLED BENEFICIARY

One of the most common problems presented to estate planning attorneys concerns disabled family members.

In many families one of the intended beneficiaries of the estate planning client is disabled; suffering from either profound physical or emotional disabilities. The client wants to make provision for his disabled relative; but does not want to impede the flow of public or private benefits to which the disabled beneficiary is entitled.

As you are probably already aware, the availability of public benefits for disabled persons varies, depending upon the nature of the program. Some programs, such as Medicare for those over age 65 and special education programs, for disabled children, are available regardless of the amount of personal resources available to an individual. Others, such as Medicaid and Aid to Families with

Dependent Children, are available only to those individuals who meet certain eligibility requirements based upon financial need.

The problem for many clients is that, while they wish to create a fund for the benefit of disabled relative in order to be able to provide that relative with "enhancements" to ordinary living which are not provided by public or private benefits; merely the establishment of such a fund, by itself, may disqualify the intended beneficiary from participation in the eligibility required program which supplies many of that beneficiaries basic needs.

The question often presented is:

How can I structure a benefit for my child which will allow him to experience some of the "nicer" things in life which subsidy programs do not provide, without disqualifying him form the benefits he receives from such programs?

This is an area of estate planning where it is crucial to obtain the advice of a skilled estate planning professional in the state of intended beneficiary's residence.

While many of the benefits to which a disabled beneficiary may be entitled are federal in nature, most of these types of programs are operated at the local level by state agencies. Thus the eligibility requirements usually vary from state to state. Only by obtaining advice from a professional knowledgeable in the requirements of the state which administers the benefits received by your intended beneficiary can you be reasonably certain that your desire to provide "extras" for such beneficiary will not, in reality, cause him harm.

This having been said, let me discuss some general principles of drafting for the benefit of disabled beneficiaries.

First: A trust is usually the best way to provide for such a beneficiary.

Any outright gift directly to the disabled person will probably trigger the need for the establishment of a conservatorship. After all, in all probability, the individual's disability may well legally or physically prevent him from signing his own name. Moreover, the direct gift to such a beneficiary, even if he can execute his signature, may well result in the benefit being expended inappropriately by the beneficiary, in a manner not reasonably well-calculated to benefit him in the long run.

If you have read the previous chapters of this book, you already know the substantial disadvantages to the establishment of a conservatorship. If you haven't, I refer you to those chapters now.

When an intended beneficiary is disabled, great care must be utilized in drafting the terms of the trust provisions dealing with the administration of the disabled beneficiary's intended benefit. Some of the more common provisions which must be reviewed, in light of a beneficiary's disability include the following:

Choice of Trustee:

It is often advisable to provide for co-trustees to deal with the assets earmarked for a disabled beneficiary. This is particularly the case where family members are not sufficiently financially savvy to make good trustees. The problem is that when an intended beneficiary is disabled, the variety of circumstances encountered during the course of trust administration normally greatly increase. This oftentimes results in trust companies not wishing to serve as the sole trustee in such circumstances. If the family is not blessed with good financial managers, the best course is to provide for co-trustees with delineated areas of responsibility; the trust company to financially manage assets in trust; a family member to exercise discretion regarding the distribution of principal and income of the trust share to or for the benefit of the disabled beneficiary. The trust company will not object to this polarized authority, but may well be happy to serve under such terms, instead.

Trustee Powers and Discretions:

As a general rule, the trustee serving in this situation is going to need much more discretionary power than the trustee serving under different circumstances. The distribution of income and principal, for example, should be discretionary with the trustee, not mandatory, even if such mandate is restricted. In fact, restrictions on discretion are generally ill-advised. A broad breadth of discretion is needed for several reasons: the nature of the beneficiary's disability may require imaginative application of income or assets in order to be truly for his benefit; by giving a trustee broad discretion over the distribution of income and principal, you better insulate the trustee from compulsion by some state agency from distributing in order to "spend down" the benefits in trust in order to re-qualify a disabled beneficiary for receipt of benefits after a court has determined that the benefits count against the beneficiary's eligibility standards. Likewise, it is a good idea to stay away from granting authority to distribute trust benefits for the disabled beneficiary's "health", maintenance" or support.

In fact it is better to specifically forbid the trustee to expend trust income or assets for these purposes.

It is also, as a general proposition, advisable to not make the benefit for the disabled beneficiary's exclusive benefit. By identifying a class of beneficiaries which includes the disabled beneficiary and providing the trustee with discretion as to the allocation and distribution of the trust benefits, from time to time, you may well successfully prevent a state agency's argument that the disabled beneficiary is entitled to a portion of the trust benefit. Obviously, if such beneficiary is not entitled to a portion of the trust, the creation and funding of the trust, in and of itself, cannot cause a specific portion's dedication to the disabled beneficiary and a required spend down for the disabled beneficiary of such portion prior to the recommencement of public or other private benefits to him.

By and large it is not advisable to fund a trust of this type through inter vivos gift. If the trust provides for Crummey powers, the notice and provision of the Crummey right to the disabled beneficiary (through his guardian) may well cause a legitimate claim that the disabled beneficiary had an outright exclusive right to some portion of the trust property and income.

Many states have, by case law and/or statute provided prescribed manners by which individuals can provide tangible benfits to disabled persons without causing disqualification from benefits provided to those who meet restricted economic standards.

Missouri has provided two different mechanisms to make such provisions.

In Tidrow v. Director, Missouri State Division of Family Services 688 S.W.2d 9 (Mo.App., e.d. 1985) a Missouri appeals court laid out certain guidelines, which, if followed, can result in the ability to make gifts for the benefit of a disabled beneficiary without causing him to be excluded from an eligibility required benefit. In Missouri this case has resulted in a drafting technique commonly known as a "Tidrow Trust".

A Tidrow Trust usually provides most, if not all of the following characteristics:

- Spendthrift Provisions which preclude a beneficiary from alienating (transferring) his interest in the trust and which specifically provides that a creditor of the beneficiary cannot attach the funds held in trust;

- Payment of income and principal from the trust to or for the disabled beneficiary is completely at the trustee's discretion;

- The purpose of the trust is to provide for the disabled beneficiary's "reasonable comfort" throughout his remaining life.

- ♦ The disabled beneficiary is not the sole beneficiary. For example, a sibling might be included as a discretionary beneficiary so long as a discretionary distribution to such nondisabled beneficiary would not jeopardize the disabled beneficiary's welfare;

- ♦ Residuary beneficiaries are person(s) other than the disabled beneficiary.

Under the case law of the state of Missouri, if a trust is drafted in such a manner as to include the just described characteristics, the establishment and funding of the trust will not cause the income or assets of the trust to be "available" to the beneficiary (as that term is used in federal law). Because these assets and income are not considered available to the disabled beneficiary, the trusts income and assets will not cause exclusion of the applicant from participation in subsidized programs.

Missouri has also created a statutory mechanism to allow a disabled beneficiary to receive benefits from third persons without causing disqualification from subsidized benefits.

The MISSOURI FAMILY TRUST FUND

This statute provides for the creation of a trust to which contributions may be made upon behalf of a disabled person. After contribution to the fund, the trust establishes a bookkeeping account upon behalf of the disabled individual and into such account is noted the gifts made to the trust on account of that disabled beneficiary.

A donor may also designate a "co-trustee" to serve with the permanent fund trustees to oversee the management of the disabled beneficiary's fund share. The co-trustee and the fund trustees are directed to agree upon an annual amount of income and principal with which to provide the disabled beneficiary noncash benefits. In the event that these parties cannot agree, there is an arbitration procedure established so that disagreement will not prevent the disabled beneficiary from receiving benefits from the trust fund.

A donor may revoke his gift to the fund and, if none of the fund's income or principal has yet been distributed to the beneficiary, 100% is returned to the donor. If distributions of benefit have been made to the disabled beneficiary, then the donor is entitled to a return of 90% of his contribution less the value of the benefits provided to the disabled beneficiary by the fund. The amount not returned to the donor pursuant to this formula is distributed to the charitable trust which is an account entry of the fund.

The acting co-trustee can withdraw the gift made for a disabled beneficiary's benefit from the fund and, upon notice of such intent to withdraw, the fund will distribute the above described amounts to a successor, independent trust established for the beneficiary's benefit with the otherwise undistributed portion going to the charitable trust.

If a disabled beneficiary's residence is removed from the state of Missouri, or for other reasons, becomes disqualified to receive state services, the fund shall distribute to a successor trust for the beneficiary's benefit 90% of the gift less the value of the benefits already distributed to the disabled beneficiary; if at the time of such disqualification the disabled beneficiary had been a beneficiary of the fund for less than five years. If the disabled beneficiary has been a participant of the fund for more than five years, then the successor trust is entitled to a return of 75% of the contribution less the value of benefits provided to the beneficiary from the fund. Again, the non-distributable portion is held upon the books in the charitable fund.

Should the designated beneficiary die before receipt of any of fund benefits, the fund will distribute the contribution to such person as the donor has designated. The undistributed income will be distributed to the charitable trust. If the disabled beneficiary has received benefit from the fund, 75% of the contribution less the value of benefits distributed from the fund to that beneficiary shall be distributed to the donor designated beneficiary with the balance distributed to the charitable trust.

The charitable trust is administered as a separate account within the family fund. The fund portion attributable to the charitable trust is utilized to provide benefits to persons who are eligible for state provided services and have no immediate family members or whose family members, in the opinion of the fund's trustees have no ability to make contributions to the fund upon behalf of the disabled individual; and thereby provide additional benefits to such individuals.

If provision is made for a disabled beneficiary's benefit through the Missouri Family Fund; regardless of the total value of the individual's account, the maintenance of such account upon his behalf by the family fund will not cause the loss of state subsidized benefits. Moreover the contributions to the fund made upon the individuals behalf will not be required to be spent down for the types of services or benefits provided to those who maintain the eligibility standards for publicly subsidized benefits, but for the family fund account.

The Missouri Family Fund is a relatively innovative and new method for allowing gifting to disabled individuals so as to provide for the nice "extras" of life (beyond subsidized services), without causing disqualification for Medicaid or other subsidy.

It should be noted, however, that one cannot be the donor/beneficiary of a Missouri Family Fund account and thereby qualify for state subsidized programs while otherwise exceeding the eligibility requirements.

It should also be noted that Tidrow Trusts cannot be established by a present asset owner in order to shield his own assets from spend down requirements imposed by Missouri law.

CONCLUSION:

Supplemental Social Security (SSI) is a federal program. Medicaid, is a federal program operated in conjunction with each individual state. Each state is allowed to create its own set of rules regarding its administration of the Medicaid program. While the state cannot be more generous then the federal law (it can't make it easier to qualify) it can make it much harder.

Because of this fact Medicaid is intensely state law specific. As always, readers are advised to consult with a qualified estate planning attorney located in the jurisdiction of the intended disabled beneficiary's residence in order to determine how to best structure benefits for such beneficiary which are meant to enhance the quality of such individual's life, above that provided by subsidized programs.

CHAPTER EIGHT

PLANNING FOR YOUR OWN DISABILITY

When attempting to plan for your own, future disability, the rules are substantially different than when planning how to transfer family wealth for the benefit of a disabled child or grandchild.

While in the last chapter we presumed that the disabled beneficiary had already qualified for Medicaid and we desired to prevent disqualification; when discussing Medicaid qualification for oneself, those eligibility requirements are all important.

You see, most people, even young people, have acquired some assets that they wish to protect by planning. As we shall soon see, having almost any assets will prevent a person from qualifying to receive Medicaid, should he become substantially disabled.

As is often the case in this book, the specifics utilized to explain the process are those applicable in the state of Missouri. While the numbers may vary from state to state, the basic principles do not.

THE QUALIFICATION TESTS

In order to qualify for Medicaid there are two "means tests" you must pass:

An Income Test and Asset Test

The Income Test:

Missouri is one of the most punitive states in the union when it comes to allowing individuals to avail themselves of the benefits of Medicaid. While the specific values are those applicable in the state of Missouri, the general discussion as to the structure of Medicaid and the techniques most often used to enhance qualification for Medicaid subsidies is applicable in every state.

In Missouri in 2014 an individual can receive monthly income of no more than $ 2,931 and still qualify for Medicaid. But what if your monthly nursing home bill is more than that? Remember, the statewide average monthly cost of a nursing home is $ 4,563.

In Missouri, you are allowed to keep $40 of your monthly income. This is called a Personal Needs Allowance. All of your other monthly income must be assigned to the nursing home and to the extent that your monthly income is less than your nursing home, Medicaid will pick up the difference. (Assuming you also pass the asset test.)

The Asset Test:

In Missouri a single Medicaid applicant can have no more than $999 of "Countable Assets" and still qualify for Medicaid.

"Countable Assets" include all of your bank accounts, C.D.s, brokerage accounts, mutual funds, annuities, IRAs, 401Ks, the cash value of life insurance, real estate that is not your primary residence, business interests and any other asset that can be converted to cash. inheritance interests are included as well.

Even if you hold such assets in a revocable living trust, Medicaid will count them.

Certain assets are "non-countable".

This means that even though you own the following types of assets, you can still qualify for Medicaid.

The greatest non-countable asset is your home.

Medicaid allows you to retain your principal residence (and all of the land that is contiguous with it and any other buildings on that land). Contiguous means that the other land touches the boundary of the lot on which your home sits. If a public road separates one lot from the residential lot, it is still considered contiguous by Medicaid.

Your home is non-countable if at the time you make a Medicaid application you are residing there or if you are not living in your home because of your disability and you are retaining your home in the hope that you will someday be able to return to it. This ability to return is limited to a two year period. Also, to the extent that your home has an equity of more than $500,000 the excess value is countable.

You can also exclude the value of certain household goods and personal effects, such as one engagement ring, one wedding ring, and necessary medical equipment.

You are also allowed to have one motor vehicle, regardless of value.

Prepaid Burial Contracts are likewise exempt, regardless of value so long as they are irrevocable and not assignable to anyone else. Burial spaces such as cemetery plots (even if for other family members) are not counted either.

If an asset is not on the list I have just described as "non-countable" owning such assets to the extent that the value exceeds $ 999 will disqualify an applicant from receiving Medicaid.

Married Individuals

If you are married and your spouse does not need to be in a nursing home, too, the rules are a bit different, because Medicaid realizes that the "community spouse" needs income and assets to live on, notwithstanding the "institutional spouse's" need for Medicaid.

The Income Test

The income of the community spouse is never considered!

So, if a nondisabled spouse receives $4,000 in monthly income (pension, social security and required distributions from IRAs) none of that is considered in determining whether his spouse qualifies for Medicaid.

How Medicaid determines whose income is whose is simple. It is determined by whose name is on the check. So if the IRA distribution is made in the sole name of the plan participant (the IRA owner) as required by federal law, and that individual is the community spouse, that check won't count. If the check is made out to both spouses, then ½ counts to each spouse.

If the community spouse's regular living expenses are greater than his/her regular income, Medicaid will allow some part of the institutional spouse's income to be used by the community spouse to pay his regular bills.

This is called the "Community Spouse Resource Allowance".

An Example:

Bill's monthly income is $ 3,000. Mary's income is $ 900. Bill is in a nursing home. How much, if any, of Bill's monthly income is Mary allowed to keep?

Start with Bill's income-	$3,000
Bill's Personal Needs Allowance	(40)
Bill's health insurance	(150)
Under Missouri law	
Next we subtract Mary's income	(900)
	$1,910

The Maximum Monthly Maintenance needs allowance for 2014 is $2,931.

Thus, in our example, Mary can keep $1,910 of Bill's monthly income.

The Asset Test

Medicaid also allows the community spouse to have assets in excess of the $999 individual limit. This excess amount of asset value is called the "Community Spouse Resource Allowance."

In 2014 this allowance is $117,240.

However, unlike with the income test, all of the couple's assets, regardless how titled, count towards the limit.

So, if (looking at Bill and Mary again) their joint countable assets are of a value of $150,000 and Mary has an IRA in her own name of $50,000, Bill will NOT QUALIFY for Medicaid, because their total assets exceed Mary and Bill's respective individual allowances of $999 and this year Resource Allowance of $117,240.00.

If however, their total countable assets had been within this year's allowance amount, Bill could qualify for Medicaid, although title to the assets would have to be transferred out of Joint names to Mary's name, alone.

The Curse of Reclamation

Remember when we talked about non-countable assets? You will note that I have referred to these assets as non-countable and have not used the commonly used term "exempt".

There is a good reason for this.

While it is true that ownership of non-countable assets will not prevent qualification for Medicaid, those assets are not truly exempt from any discussion about Missouri Medicaid.

This is because of "RECLAMATION"!

The Medicaid laws in Missouri state that, although non-countable assets do not count against the maximum limits one can have and still qualify for Medicaid, that does not mean that they are exempt from risk of loss to the Medicaid system.

Rather, the law provides that when you die, the state has a lien against those non-countable assets to the extent of the amount of Medicaid payments the state has made on your account.

SO: If Bill had stayed in a nursing home for two years, subsidized by Missouri Medicaid, at a monthly cost of $5,000, at the time of his death, Medicaid is owed $120,000. The state will place a lien on those non-countable assets titled in Bill's sole name and can even open a Probate Estate in order to force the sale of those assets in order to reclaim the Medicaid the state has paid.

There is one benefit that Missouri allows in reclamation that many states do not. If the non-countable property was in joint name (as was the case with Bill and Mary's home) and Mary survives Bill and is not institutionalized herself; the house will not be subject to reclamation fro Bills Medicaid payments.

So, given all of these complex qualification and reclamation rules what can one do protect assets and income from nursing home costs?

Most people figure the way to solve the problem is to simply give everything away before making a Medicaid application.

The problem with this thinking is IT DOESN'T WORK.

TRANSFER PENALTIES

Federal law provides that there is a "disqualification" period of up to 60 months (5 years) if you simply give away your assets.

So, if your plan is "Give it away!" in place of

"Spend it all!", just recognize that this could lead to your being very poor and totally disqualified from nursing home benefits for a very long time.

When you make an application for Medicaid there is a question on the application that asks if you have given anything away within 60 months (5 years) of the date of the Medicaid Application.

If the answer is "Yes", the applicant is disqualified from receiving Medicaid for a period of time determined by a formula.

That formula starts with the value of the assets that you have given away and divides that value by a state derived figure, the Divestment Penalty Divisor (for 2014 that number is $4,563 per month).

An Example: Tom's health is in decline and he can see the need for nursing home care in his immediate future. His total countable asset value is $ 300,000, which he transfer to his children. Two years later he has to go to the nursing home and he makes a Medicaid Application.

$300,000/4,563 = 65.75 months.

Using the formula above we see that, although he has no assets, Tom cannot receive the benefits of Medicaid for more than 5 years because he gave his assets away.

When does the disqualification period start?

As a result of recent changes in the law, the disqualification period starts when the Medicaid application is made and the applicant, if single, has less than $ 999 (except for the value he gave away).

Since the Medicaid application was made two years after Tom transferred his assets, the disqualification period of more than five years does not start until that time, meaning that Tom has been effectively disqualified for more than seven years from the date of the transfers.

IS THERE ANYTHING YOU CAN DO?

Every Medicaid applicant's situation is different. What may work for one family may not for another. Because Medicaid qualification is so complicated it is essential that the attorney with whom you plan is knowledgeable about this complex area of the law.

A FEW ASSET SAVING TECHNIQUES

"CRISIS PLANNING"

If you find yourself in the situation where the prospect of a long term nursing home stay is immediate because of a sudden onset of disability, here are several techniques an attorney might suggest.

CONVERT COUNTABLE ASSETS TO NON-COUNTABLE ASSETS

Because your car and home are usually not countable, one "emergency technique" is to invest countable assets on non-countable ones.

>Buy a new car;
>Remodel the bath or kitchen;
>Pre-pay your funeral and burial.

"HALF A LOAF" CONVERSION

In this strategy you give away just enough asset value such that the amount you keep will pay for your nursing home stay during the disqualification period.

"LONG TERM PLANNING"

The biggest problem with "crisis planning" is that it always results in a substantial loss of assets to the Medicaid system. Even in the first technique, you have to remember that you are only deferring the nursing home bill, not avoiding it. Remember, the bill comes due upon your death because of RECLAMATION.

If you are truly concerned about protecting yourself and your family from the devastating cost of nursing home care, the best advice I can give is:

PLAN IN ADVANCE!

You could invest in long term care insurance, but if you are reading this and are over the age of 60, you will probably find the premiums exorbitant to the point that such insurance is not a realistic option for you.

What else might you do?

REMEMBER:

Medicaid looks back FIVE YEARS to see if there have been any disqualifying transfers.

Obviously, the trick is to make such a transfer more than five years before need arises.

The problem of course, is determining to whom to transfer the results of your life's work.

Most people, if not confronted by a crisis nursing home admission, are reluctant to give away everything they have worked their whole life to acquire. I have had more than one client tell me:

I'll give up control of my assets when they can pry my cold, dead hand off of them.

Obviously, for people who have this philosophy, the idea of giving their assets away, even to their children, is not an appealing prospect. And, there are valid reasons not to give your assets to your children with no strings attached, with the hope that they will give them back , in whole or in part, should the need arise.

If you give title to your assets to your children, the assets become theirs. This means that you can't make them give them back. But let's assume that is not a problem in your family.

There are still the problems we discussed in previous chapters. The children may die before you, causing the assets to pass to other, less trustworthy beneficiaries. Or they could pass to minors subject to a conservatorship under the control of the probate judge who will only allow them to be used for the "underage" beneficiary to whom they have devolved by virtue of your child's unanticipated death.

In similar fashion your adult child could become disabled himself and be faced with the same "spend down" problems you seek to cure for yourself.

And, of course, if your trusted child holds title to the assets, they are always at risk to his or her own divorce or creditors.

But suppose I could show you a way to "give away" your assets and still retain control of them, long before the "crisis" arises. And what's more, keep them protected from all of the risks I just enumerated?

Here is a long term strategy that I have found clients find very appealing:

Create an Irrevocable Trust and transfer your assets to the trust long before the need for nursing home care arises.

Unlike the revocable living trust we have previously discussed, once you have established the terms of an irrevocable trust, you cannot change them.

However, when you really think about it, if you create a trust that states that the beneficiary of the assets held in trust are your children, who won't receive any of the assets as a matter of right until after your death, what really are the odds that you will want to change these terms?

So, let's create a revocable trust that provides that during your life, you are entitled to receive all of the income generated each month by the trust but that use of the principal (the assets you transferred to the trust) are reserved for the benefit of your children or other loved ones when you die.

However, let's also provide that if, in the discretion of your trustee, he or she believes that one or more of your death beneficiaries has need of principal of the trust the trustee can invade the principal for that their benefit.

Now, why would we want to provide that last part?

This latter provision is your "escape hatch" whereby you can access principal of the trust, if you should really need it.

If, for some reason, the monthly income generated by the trust assets do not meet your needs, you can request the trustee to make a discretionary invasion of the principal of the trust to a trusted child, who then can make a gift of the amount you need to you.

Because of the changes in the estate tax laws we have already discussed, there will not be any gift tax on the "gift" from your chosen beneficiary back to you.

Many of my clients who fear that they will have to someday go to a nursing home and lose everything that they worked their whole life to acquire find that this irrevocable trust technique is a safe way to protect their assets from Medicaid spend down requirements.

CONCLUSION:

The laws governing nursing home subsidies via Medicaid are complex and confusing. To plan to protect against the devastating cost of nursing home care takes the skill of an attorney who knows the "ins and outs" of the Medicaid qualification process.

While there are techniques to salvage family assets in the event of an unanticipated nursing home "Crisis", even the best techniques will usually result in substantial loss of assets.

If you fear the risk of a future long term stay in a nursing home, the wise course to follow is to plan well in advance for the possibility.

A planning technique such as the use of an Irrevocable Medicaid Qualification Trust can be an essential part of your estate plan in order to protect your assets for your own use and for the benefit of your loved ones in the event that a nursing home stay is in your future.

CHAPTER NINE

HOW TO CHOOSE YOUR ESTATE PLANNING ATTORNEY

Now that you know a little more about basic estate planning, how do you go about choosing an attorney to help you actually draft the plan which will best protect your family's interests?

While there are many good attorneys located in any town, the number of good estate planning attorneys is substantially smaller. While every attorney who graduated from law school instinctively believes that he/she can write a will, the fact of the matter is that all too few are actually skilled in the art of estate planning. Why is this so?

First of all, many attorneys graduate from law school without ever having taken a course in basic wills and trusts, let alone estate tax planning. The sad fact is that many law schools do not require such courses as a condition for graduation. having read this book, you know as much or more than many practicing attorneys. This is not to say that those attorneys are not skilled in other areas of practice. Quite frankly, if you came to me to seek representation in a lawsuit arising out of catastrophic injury, I would refer you to any number of highly skilled plaintiff personal injury attorneys and I would candidly admit that your best interests most certainly would not lie in my representation of you.

Why ?

Because, I haven't tried a personal injury lawsuit in over twenty years. Even though I took torts and trial practice and civil procedure in law school, those classes taken a quarter of a century ago just are not going to prove that helpful in representing you today. In like manner, lawyers who do not engage in estate planning on a daily basis are probably ill suited to meet your estate planning needs. This is particularly the case where you are fortunate to have an estate large enough in value to possible be subjected to estate taxation. The tax laws (or some component or interpretation thereof) change or are refined on a literally daily basis.

How can someone who does not keep abreast of these rapidly changing laws adequately protect your interests ?

It is a sad fact that law, like medicine, is a

practice which increasingly requires limitation in scope. The days where the same lawyer could competently try your injury action, represent your corporation, negotiate your real estate or employment contract, properly plan your estate and draft appropriate documents and fix your son's traffic ticket are long gone. Law, like everything else, now develops upon too rapid a pace for an attorney to keep properly informed upon all aspects of the law. This is particularly trust in the area of estate tax planning.

The tax court through its decisions and the IRS through its interpretive bulletins, letter rulings, proposed regulations and technical advice memoranda continually develop and refine estate tax law on a near daily basis. Unless a practitioner is particularly focused upon this area of law on a daily basis, the odds are good that the law will pass that practitioner by and his advice will be outmoded.

How can you determine if an attorney is well skilled in the area of estate planning.

You can always look for professional affiliations which will show that he/she has an active interest in the subject.

The Martindale-Hubbell Law Directory is a reference book found at most public libraries. It is a listing of attorneys and law firms by geographic location. It includes in each listing an identification of the types of law practiced and provides a biographical sketch of each attorney. In those biographical sketches are included the professional accomplishments of note and professional affiliations maintained by the attorney. Look there to see if the attorney belongs to the ABA or his/her state or local bar association's probate and/or trust law section. If the attorney is located in a large metropolitan area, see if he belongs to the Estate Planning Counsel located in that city.

A very select group of estate planning attorneys belong to a national society of estate planners called the American College of Trust and Estate Planning Counsel (ACTEC). It should be noted, however, that ACTEC is somewhat of a closed group (admission is upon nomination and election by the membership, and tends to favor attorneys who practice in large "silk-stocking" law firms that represent international corporations and bill accordingly.)

Interview your proposed estate planning attorney.

How do you do that ?

After all, you know virtually nothing about estate planning and the lawyer, even if not an expert must know something. How can you avoid being fooled?

First of all, don't be intimidated!

As noted above, it may well be that the attorney really doesn't know as much as you (assuming you've read this book to this point).

Second: for most people it is really quite simple to apply a quick litmus test to determine whether your proposed attorney knows at least the basics of estate planning. Don't make the mistake which most clients make in the area of estate planning: self diagnosis and prescription.

If you didn't feel well would you go to your doctor and say:

I have been running a slight fever; my sinuses feel congested, I am achy; my nose is running and I am coughing and sneezing. Therefore, I want you to write prescription or amoxicillin, 50 milligrams to be taken three times daily.

Of course not. Yet, when seeking advice regarding the preservation and distribution of everything one has worked his/her entire life to acquire, it is not uncommon for that person to go to an attorney and say:

I want you to write a will for me

and my family.

In uttering that sentence, the client has unwittingly self diagnosed his legal problem (the need for estate planning based upon his/her particular life situation) and self prescribed the cure (a will as the appropriate estate plan).

When you self diagnose and prescribe in this manner, you are depriving yourself of the benefit of exactly that which you seek: the analysis and professional advice of a trained practitioner regarding a substantial financial investment; everything you own. You are also depriving yourself of the ability to determine if the attorney you have chosen actually is worthy of the confidence you are reposing in him.

Instead of making a declaration when you see the attorney, ask a simple question:

What are my estate planning needs ?

See how the attorney answers.

Does he or she ask you for a disclosure of your assets and liabilities ?

Does he or she inquire as to your specific family situation; (i.e.) the identity and birthdates of your children?

Does he inquire whether your present spouse (if you are married) is your first? If not, are there children to consider which are not born of your present marriage? If so, does he inquire as to whose children they are?

Does he inquire regarding your present income level and your anticipated retirement income needs?

Does he inquire as to whether you or any of your family members suffer from any medical or other condition which would require special planning in order to best protect that individual.

Does he inquire as to whether there are "special circumstances" regarding any family member about which you are concerned?

Does he inquire as to whether you have retirement benefits assets, their value and if you wish to distribute them differently than your other assets?

A skilled estate planner will ask all of these questions, and many more, in order to determine the estate plan which will best protect your assets from probate costs as well as estate and income taxes; and carry out your distributive desires.

Does the attorney provide you alternative planning choices?

There is usually more than one way to accomplish estate planning goals and the choice of plan often is determined by particular predispositions of the client.

And now the acid test:

Does the attorney even mention the existence of a revocable living trust as a planning alternative?

If the attorney does not even mention the existence of a trust as an estate planning tool you might wish to use; and your total asset value from all sources is in excess of $100,000 , you should run, not walk from that attorney's office.

With few exceptions, if your estate is worth more than $100,000 , it will probably be less expensive, overall, for you to use a revocable living trust as the primary tool for the planning of your estate than any other.

While the cost of drafting trusts varies from state to state (and from attorney to attorney, for that matter); unless your attorney's law firm customarily represents fortune five hundred companies or defense contractors (where hammers and toilet seats cost $350-$500), those so-called "silk stocking" firms; the cost for preparation of a revocable living trust and its related, necessary documents and the advice required at the time of a Settlor's disability or death will be far less than the fees generated in a probate proceeding; and will probably be the best method to protect your assets and insure their distribution to your intended beneficiaries in the manner and at the time which you desire.

Thus, if your attorney doesn't, at the very least, mention the existence of the availability of a trust as an estate planning tool and suggest its possible use, either one of two situations exist; neither of which is in your best interest.

Either:

The Attorney doesn't know much about estate planning

Or

The Attorney is more concerned about his pocket than yours.

Why do I say this ?

As previously noted, attorneys who are sound practitioners in other areas of the law, may not have ever taken a law school course in trusts, estate taxation or estate planning, nor educated himself after graduation by professional education programs which are available to attorneys. While almost every attorney inherently believes that he/she has the ability to properly draft a will (even though that is not necessarily a particularly valid assumption); most attorneys who know nothing or little about trusts quite rightly have a substantial fear of them. They, at the least, know that they seem long, complicated and "tricky" to draft; and they, quite rightly, fear exposure to that (shudder) most hated of terms professional liability (that's malpractice to just us folks) if the trust is improperly drafted.

Surprisingly, most attorneys don't have this same fear about writing wills, although the risk to the untrained and unwary is just as great.

Accordingly, since "every lawyer knows how to write a will" that unskilled practitioner will be happy to write one for you; oftentimes with the best of intentions. One of the sad truths about attorneys and malpractice is that when they commit it, more often than not, they are not aware that they have.

So, if you are seeking advice from an old family friend who has tried your car wreck case and fixed little Timmy's ticket and he tells you, without more, that he will be happy to write a will for you and your spouse which will dandily take care of your needs; don't necessarily sever your friendship, now suspecting him to be a crook. He may not know any better ! But, whatever you do, don't, for the sake of friendship and fear of offending, have him draft that will without first seeking the advice of another attorney for a "second opinion" as to whether a will is really the best planning document for you and your family.

Why would an attorney ever put his best financial interest ahead of yours and why would the suggestion of a will accomplish this goal ?

I'll leave the answer to the first part of the question to your own imagination. (You can probably think of at least ten "Lawyer" jokes to insert at this point).

The answer to the second part of the question is quite simple.

If you have ever had a will prepared, were you surprised at how little its preparation cost ?

(Don't snicker. Bear in mind that the purpose of the document is to effect the distribution of everything you have worked your whole life to acquire. Now compare the cost of that will to a big screen TV, which while perhaps you will use more frequently, probably does not have such an impact upon your children's lives).

The reason is quite simple:

Wills are to attorneys what bananas and chickens are to grocers.

(My dad owned a market.)

They are loss leaders.

For the uninitiated, a loss leader is a product advertised for sale a low cost (maybe, even at below cost and, hence at a loss) in order to lure customers into the store and thereby cause other purchases, while there to purchase the loss leader, which will generate the store's owner a far greater profit and which he would not have sold to the customer had he not been lured to the store by the advertised bargain.

How is a Will a loss leader ? Simple.

The attorney will write the will for a nominal fee in order to be able to have the opportunity to probate that will at the time of your death and thereby obtain the substantially greater probate service fee.

Many general practitioner attorneys refer to the wills that they have drafted as their retirement plans. In drafting the will, the Attorney knows that there is a great likelihood that at the time of your death there will have to be a probate. Remember, a will is nothing more than a road map for the probate judge to follow in the course of a decedent estate administration.

If you already have a will, take it out and look at it. See if the name of the attorney who drafted the will does not appear upon the binder. Does it appear there merely because the attorney is proud of his/her work or so that you won't forget his name in the event that you want to revise the will in the future? Those could be reasons for its appearance. But the more likely reason is that the attorney wants your beneficiaries to know who wrote the will. The reasoning is that the beneficiaries will take the will back to the lawyer who drafted it for probate. After all, he's the one who drafted it and therefore spoke with dad and really knows what dad wanted done, right? Often times, you will find the name of the attorney not only upon the binder of the will; but in the body of the will, as well. the language will look like the following:

> In making this, my Last Will and Testament, I have relied upon the sage advise of my friend and attorney, Joe Blow in whom I place my trust and confidence.

Do you think that sends a pointed enough message to the heirs as to whom should be employed to probate the will?

How about this one:

I direct my personal representative, in the probate administration of this, my Last Will and Testament, to employ my friend and attorney, Joe Blow, as attorney for the estate and provide that his compensation shall be that as provided by law.

If you read that passage in your father's will, do you think that you would be legally bound, as a precondition of your appointment as personal representative of your father's estate, to hire Joe Blow as the estate's attorney. Not so surprisingly, most people think that such a direction is legally binding upon them. The reality in most states is that the personal representative is free to choose any attorney to represent him in the administration of a probate estate, to be probated according to a will with such language. The language, in fact and law, is not binding.

Obviously, the reason for the insertion of such language in such wills is to give the draftsman a leg up on the competition in obtaining the right to probate the will and earn (?) the fees generated thereby.

An older attorney of my acquaintance consistently greets me, when meeting in the court house with the inquiry:

> "Still drafting those trusts?"

When I respond:

> "Still drafting those wills?"

His response is uniform:

Sure, Robby (his young son who is also a lawyer) still will need work long after I'm gone.

In closing this part of the discussion I offer this reminder;

> You really have to like your lawyer
> to want to make him one of your heirs!

Other question you should be sure to ask

In addition to the above, there are some other questions which you should always ask the attorney before engaging his services.

Always ask the amount of the fee and how the fee is computed.

You wouldn't engage a contractor to build an addition to your house without knowing the total cost in advance, would you ? Then why would you give an attorney free rein to charge whatever he wanted after the documents were prepared for you?

Don't be afraid to ask the attorney how much the agreed upon plan is going to cost. A good planner will anticipate your question and tell you his fee and explain its basis before you ask.

Ask the attorney what portion of his practice is devoted to Estate Planning and how many plans he has drafted within the past 12 months.

As you should realize by now, estate planning can be a complex proposition. Not only does a lawyer have to have been educated in the discipline; he has to keep himself educated in an area of law which literally changes daily.

If the attorney tells you that estate planning does not comprise the majority of his practice, you will be better served finding an attorney who is primarily an estate planner. In this way you can be reasonably assured that the attorney is current in his knowledge of this area of the law.

Ask how long it will take to prepare your plan. Ask to set the Appointment for your Return.

One of the most common client complaints, when trying to obtain estate planning services, is that it takes forever for the attorney to complete the project.

This complaint is most commonly expressed when the attorney practices many areas of law.

After all, if your attorney commonly spends his day at the courthouse, when do you think he has time to analyze your estate and prepare your planning documents?

As a general rule, for a basic living trust estate plan, the total time, from agreement of the plan's terms, to execution of finished documents, should take no longer than three weeks. If it takes longer than this to prepare a basic plan, the odds are good that the attorney does not engage in estate planning as his primary professional avocation.

A good estate planning attorney will want to set the appointment for your return to execute the plan documents as soon as possible. After all, he won't receive his whole fee until you are satisfied with the plan. Thus, he has every incentive to complete your project as quickly as reasonably possible.

By the same token, be wary if the planner can have your plan ready in too brief a time period.

Remember, this is a complex topic and we are talking about everything you own. Even a simple plan must be drafted and reviewed by the attorney. Too short a waiting period indicates either business is slow or a lack of care by the practitioner in the preparation of your plan.

The one question not to ask.

Don't ask for draft documents!

They just slow the planning process down.

Requesting draft documents is the equivalent of a car purchaser kicking the tires.

A good estate planner is going to review the pertinent portions of your documents with you at the second conference, when you sign them. If he has misinterpreted your desires, that fact will be determined at the meeting, before you are called upon sign them.

While you might desire to see your architect's renderings and schematics before you start construction of your house, you will normally go through them with the architect. Why?

Absent professional training, you probably won't be able to correctly interpret whether the renderings properly reflect your desires without the aid of the architect.

The same holds true for your estate plan.

While good planners try to write your plan in user friendly English, there are accepted structures and language in a trust which are not readily understandable without the interpretive aid of the attorney.

I have found that sending draft documents to clients only encourages the client to revert to that greatest of estate planning impediments procrastination.

While we are each interested in preserving our estates for our loved ones' benefit, let's not kid ourselves; Estate Plans make for boring reading. The Trust, itself, is much like the telephone book:

It has a fascinating cast of characters; but the plot quickly gets boring.

My experience in sending drafts is that the client quickly tires of reading the document and puts it aside. Then, because he doesn't want to admit that he hasn't read it (after all he insisted on receiving the draft); he hides from his attorney. Now the plan remains uncompleted for an extended period of time, because the client doesn't want to admit that he really doesn't want to read the trust, or if he does, that he does not understand it in its entirety.

Other Pertinent Documents you should

receive:

Other than mentioning a trust; what should your estate planning attorney, at the very least, suggest ?

If you decide that you want a Will:

If, after due consideration of the relevant factors, you determine that a Will is in your best interest, your attorney, in most states, should suggest that you draft a General Durable Power of Attorney.

<u>General Durable Power of Attorney</u>

Under common law (that is, the law developed over time from our English precedential roots and the court cases of the state of residence) a power of attorney was a document the signing of which gave the grantee (the person to whom it was given) the power to perform some act upon behalf of the person who caused the power to be written. The only problem was, in the event of legal incompetence or disability, the grant of authority expired. This did not make a Power of Attorney a particularly useful tool for avoiding probate court in the event that one became disabled.

Many states, recognizing the need to provide relief from the previously discussed burdens of conservatorships to those who desired to plan ahead for the risk of disability, created statutes which provide for the ability designate a person to hold the power to deal with your assets upon your behalf when you are disabled or incompetent. These statutes provide for Durable Powers of Attorney. The durability is that the power continues or arises upon the Settlor's disability. Many states have adopted a uniform version of the Durable Power of Attorney (although in adopting the "uniform" code, the legislatures almost universally tinker with its provisions.

Remember, a Will only takes effect upon one's death. In order to successfully avoid the need for a conservatorship, in the event of disability, the best choice is to execute a Durable Power of Attorney before disability arises, giving your chosen designee the legal ability to manage you finances for you at a time when you cannot fend for yourself.

Health Care Documents

What other "basic documents" should your attorney at least mention if a Will is your planning vehicle of choice?

I strongly recommend to all my clients that they consider executing Health Care Documents. In many states these come in two varieties: a Living Will (oftentimes called a Healthcare Directive) and a Health Care Durable Power of Attorney.

Living Will

A Living Will is a document of statutory creation which allows you to legally dictate to your physician or health care provider that in certain health care situations (a terminal condition, for example) medical procedures be administered to artificially prolong death or sustain life (terminology depends upon a state's particular statute). There is a uniform act; however, at date of publication only six states had enacted some variation thereof.

In somewhat curt terminology, a Living Will tells your doctor to "pull the plug" if the suggested course of treatment is not reasonably calculated to improve your medical condition, but rather, merely prolong the process of dying. Obviously where an individuals personal beliefs do not support such a proposition, the drafting of such a document is unwarranted. As with most topics in estate planning, there is a Uniform Act. To date, only six states have adopted, in some form the Uniform Act, although many states have enacted some type of statute to allow declarations regarding life support. (See Appendix).

Durable Power of Attorney for Health Care

While the Living Will serves as an individual's personal statement regarding his desires for continued treatment when his health has devolved to the point that he/she has a terminal condition; a Durable power of Attorney for Health Care allows an individual to convey that power to another, to be exercised upon behalf of the individual at a time when he/she physically cannot make such direction. This is particularly helpful in situations where some discretion is required in the making of the decision to withhold or withdraw treatment. Unfortunately it is all too often the case that the decision as to whether to terminate treatment is not cut and dried. Rather, often there is required the exercise of some discretion or discernment, based upon the facts then presented as to whether it is in the patient's best interest to terminate treatment.

A Durable Power of Attorney for Health Care is often the best way to reasonably insure that an individual's wishes regarding continued treatment will be fulfilled. In our office, whenever we draft a Living Will, we always draft a Durable Power of Attorney for Healthcare as a companion document. Similarly, if for moral or philosophical reasons, a client does not desire a Living Will, a Durable Power of Attorney for Healthcare, will not be drafted.

Additional Basic Documents When Utilizing a Trust:

When a Trust is utilized as the primary estate planning document, what additional documents, at a minimum, should be drafted ?

Health Care Documents

Healthcare documents should be drafted, assuming that the client does not wish his/her estate value dissipated for medical care which will not substantially improve his/her medical condition, but merely prolong the act of dying.

Safety Net Documents

Durable Powers of Attorney

There are two essential safety net documents which should be drafted whenever a trust is utilized as the primary estate planning document. These documents are the Durable Power of Attorney and a Pour Over Will.

We have already discussed Durable Powers of Attorney, above. The purpose of the power, in the context of trust planning is to allow a method to continue or complete funding of the trust by re-titling of assets in the event that, should an individual become disabled, assets not yet [placed in the trust can be re-titled therein. This avoids the need for a conservatorship in the situation where, for whatever reason or lack of reason, an asset which should have been re-titled in the name of the trust has not been so re-titled and the fact is discovered after the onset of disability.

Some estate planners utilize a general power of attorney, in the trust context, while others utilize a limited power of attorney. Proponents of the use of a general power of attorney cite the possible need for additional estate planning (primarily for estate tax planning purposes in the future) at a time when the client is disabled. Proponents of the limited power tend to limit the power to a single one: the power to re-title assets into the name of the trust.

Proponents of the limited power have explained to me that it has been their experience that the general power is often times inadvertently abused. The holder of the power gets confused between executing title documents as the attorney-in-fact and as the trustee (the same individual usually holds both designations) with the result that more assets end up outside the trust than inside because of the inadvertent misuse of the power of attorney.

In this area there is no one way.

<u>Pour Over Wills</u>

Many people ask:

If I am using a trust as my primary estate planning vehicle, why do I need a Will, in addition to the trust. I thought the whole point of the trust was to avoid probate.

Doesn't a Will indicate that there will be a probate at the time of my death ?

The Pour Over Will, much like the Durable Power of Attorney, is a safety net document. It is included in the basic planning documents to hedge the risk that at the time of death, an individual still has some asset titled in his sole name. As previously noted, if at the time of death an individual holds an asset titled in his/her sole name, the title to that asset will become "locked up"; with the only key to be found in the probate court. If one dies in such a situation and has not contingently planned therefor, the result, at the end of the probate process will be inheritance through the intestacy code.

The term "Pour Over" is a quite literal description of the purpose of this contingent Will; which will be utilized only in the circumstance where; notwithstanding the creation and funding of a trust; an individual dies with an asset titled in his name. In such circumstance this Will can be utilized to insure that, having the need to be probated at this time, that it will not need to be probated again in the near future and will, in fact, be transferred into the trust for eventual distribution according to the terms of that trust.

Think of an old time pitcher and washbowl: the pitcher is the trust; the washbowl the will. After the trust is created it is filled by putting one's assets therein. If, by chance, in filling the pitcher there is spillage (improper re-titling which is not effective, for example) the asset falls into the washbowl. When the error is discovered (presumably, at the time of an individuals death) the improperly titled assets are poured over into the pitcher from the washbowl via the probate process. As noted, thereafter, actual distribution to intended beneficiaries is made from the trust according to its terms.

Again, whether utilizing a will or a trust as one's primary estate planning vehicle, if your attorney of choice does not mention the need for these additional estate planning documents; run, don't walk from his office. The failure to suggest (insist) that these additional basic documents are prepared as part of the estate plan is a good indication that the practitioner does not engage in much estate planning and that, accordingly, the risk that the main planning document is improperly drafted (or that it is not the proper primary planning document for you) is quite high.

Funding Documents

Finally, always ask the estate planning attorney if he/she is going to help you re-title your assets into the name of the trust and what additional charge there is for this additional service. Oftentimes the situation occurs that a client sees an estate planner and, after executing the planning documents, shakes hands and bids the attorney a fond adieu without having any idea as to how to re-title his assets in the trusts name or to re-designate death beneficiaries so as to integrate insurance or deferred benefit assets into the trust's name. When it strikes consciousness that he has no clue as to what he is supposed to do, the client is usually about to enter his car in the parking garage. When he goes back upstairs, asks to see his attorney briefly, and then asks the attorney,

What am I supposed to do now ?

The usual response is:

Don't worry; we can handle that for you.

We charge on an hourly basis for such services.

Our hourly fee therefore is only $200 per hour."

Suddenly, that bargain estate plan isn't so much of a bargain, anymore.

Obviously, this response is from an attorney who, notwithstanding the utilization of trusts as an estate planning tool, is still trying to maximize the fee.

Remember Living Trust Planning is a two step process:

The first step is, of course, the creation of the trust document, itself.

However, the equally important second step is the funding of the trust by re-titling of assets and re-designation of death beneficiaries.

As we have previously discussed, to allow the client to attempt to make the determination of proper re-titling and re-designation is tantamount to malpractice.

Remember, the trust only works its magic over those assets which are re-titled or re-designated into the name of the trust. To not properly oversee the re-titling and re-designation of assets will virtually assure that some asset will either end up in a probate estate, or distribute to someone other than the chosen beneficiary.

Always make sure that as part of the services to be rendered by the estate planning attorney that the supervision of re-titling and re-designation of assets is part of the services to be rendered and always checkout if there is an additional charge, beyond the planning fee, for such services !

CONCLUSION:

Not all attorneys are good estate planning attorneys. While every law school graduate just assumes that he can write a will, most understand that trust documents are more complex and mistakes in drafting can result in severe economic harm to the client; or at best, result in costly litigation.

Don't be afraid to ask any lawyer the questions I have suggested in this chapter. They will help you quickly determine if the attorney you are meeting is the right attorney to help you plan your estate.

CHAPTER TEN

MAKING THE MOST OF YOUR PLANNING CONFERENCE

In order to make the most efficient use of your time at your estate planning conference; you must prepare for it.

Listed below are the things you should think about in preparation for your conference. As you make decisions or determine that you have questions which need to be answered before you can make a decision, write down your decisions and questions. This will make your conference go smoother and will allow you maximize the value of your time with your attorney.

To whom do you wish your assets to benefit when you die?

In thinking about your potential beneficiaries,

don't worry about drafting the plan yourself. Far too many clients get caught up in the technical language of the plan. When I ask them whom they wish to benefit, they start trying to rattle off specific trust language.

The question is not that hard !

First, figure out about whom you care and the priority of that care. When thinking about potential beneficiaries, think of those whom you want to most benefit first and thereafter think about those "special" bequests, whether to individuals or entities.

For most people this is usually their kids and grandkids.

However, if your children are already well heeled such that you don't feel that they need the full benefit of your assets think about what portion you want your kids to have as a percentage of your total estate; or think about giving them an income interest only for some period of time.

When thinking about these main beneficiaries, keep asking yourself this question:

> If that beneficiary should predecease you, then to whom do you want that benefit to pass?

You must continue to ask yourself this question, in each instance until you reach the point that you have chosen an institution or individuals that you may not even personally know (Does anybody really know the identity of his fifth cousin once removed?)

Remember, the purpose of estate planning is to think about every bad thing that can happen and to plan its contingency.

After you have determined whom will inherit the bulk of your assets, determine if there is any person or entity to whom you wish to leave a "token" gift at the time of your death. It is not uncommon to wish to include as a beneficiary one's church or favorite health related charity or "the young man down the street who has always been so nice". After you have determined the identity of these beneficiaries, determine what or how much you wish them to have. If your intended benefit is large, consider giving them a percentage share, rather than a fixed sum.

Remember, specific (items) and general (money) beneficiaries receive their distribution before the residuary beneficiaries. While most people always assume that the residuary shares will be the largest, if the value of your estate recedes over time, the residuary beneficiaries may receive less the those whom you intended to only slightly benefit.

Remember, too, to decide what you want to have happen to these lesser beneficiaries' shares if they predecease you.

Think about the timing of distributions to intended beneficiaries.

If the intended beneficiary is young, it may be a good idea to defer that beneficiary's enjoyment over time and in several installments.

Likewise, if an intended beneficiary suffers from some type of disability, it might be a good idea to create special provisions for distribution of intended benefits to or for him. Most states have some provision (either by statute or case law) which will allow some sort of provision for discretionary distribution of benefits for a disabled beneficiary in such a manner that the distribution will not cause loss of state or federal subsidies to the disabled beneficiary.

If you have step children, do you want them treated the same as your own children?

Do you want your sons or daughters-in-law to benefit?

Do not generalize that your step children are the equivalent of blood kin. You must tell your attorney the specific legal relationship, if any, to your intended beneficiary so that the attorney can adequately provide for him/her. The law will exclude step children if you do not specifically make provision therefor. Similarly, unless you tell your attorney to the contrary, most will automatically treat your in-laws as outlaws and presume that you want them excluded to the benefit of your descendants. If you want your son or daughter-in-law included as a beneficiary of your assets, you must specifically tell your attorney of that desire.

Is there anyone whom you wish to exclude from participation in the enjoyment of your assets?

While we often focus upon whom to include, sometimes clients wish to exclude certain individuals who, under usual circumstances, would be included as a natural bounty of one's affection. If so, make sure that you identify any such individual.

When discussing the issue of exclusion of a particular relative, I usually discourage outright exclusion. After all, if you exclude such a person, what deterrent is there to prevent him from challenging the estate plan.

Instead, I recommend that my client consider the wealth and personal disposition of the individual he desires to exclude and then; provide for the distribution to him of the lowest amount my client reasonably believes that individual will not wish to risk losing. By joining a small yet potentially significant (to the disfavored relative) inheritance with a forfeiture provision which states that if anyone contests any aspect of the estate plan and loses such contest, such contestant will forfeit the benefit otherwise provided; more often than not, after death challenges to the plan are relatively rare.

Whom do you desire to manage your affairs for you should you become disabled ?

Make multiple choices.

The most common aspect of planning which people forget is to designate persons who will be granted legal authority over assets in the event that the owner becomes disabled. I guess to some extent that we all from time to time feel like we will live forever and never be disabled. This is not the time to make those assumptions.

Moreover, when choosing successor fiduciaries (people who will take care of your financial well being when you can't) remember what you are doing, which is:

Choosing the person(s) who will have total control of your assets; to manage them and make them grow; so that you will be adequately cared for should your disability be lengthy in time.

Many people are concerned, when choosing successor fiduciaries, that they will offend one or the other of their children if they do not appoint them as a successor fiduciary.

This is the least occurrence when you should be concerned about your children's tender sensitivities. If the person you choose to manage your affairs at times when you cannot is not fit for the job; the person who will suffer most from this poor choice is you.

Remember, always keep asking yourself the question, when choosing fiduciaries:

If he/she is unable or unwilling to manage your assets for you then whom do you wish to appoint?

I usually recommend choosing at least three alternate fiduciaries. If you do not know three people who are qualified or are willing to so serve; then you should strongly consider naming a trust company as the final alternate fiduciary; just to assure that there will be a qualified entity able to serve should the need arise.

If you don't know anything about any of the trust companies in your geographic area, ask your attorney for a recommendation and always ask him the reason behind the recommendation.

Remember, as well, that your chosen fiduciaries may have to serve for an extended period of time after your death, depending upon the terms of your plan. The point, don't choose all of your fiduciaries from your or prior generations. The odds are that they may well predecease you and leave your asset's management to people of other than your choosing.

After you have made your choices, make sure that your chosen fiduciaries are willing to so serve. Ask them. Better to know now, when making your planning choices, that your desired fiduciary really doesn't want the job.

If you have minor children, remember to choose guardians.

This is usually obvious to most individuals. In fact for younger clients, it is usually the motivating factor for planning.

Remember when deciding upon guardians that their job is to take care of the persons of your children, to be surrogate parents in your place. Financial savvy is not the primary qualification for guardians.

Remember, too, if you are divorced, that your ex-spouse, if the parent of the children in your primary custody, will automatically have the legal right to custody of the children, notwithstanding your designation of guardians.

After you have identified all of the above, put your information in order for review by your attorney.

For each individual you have identified, supply a current residence address, birth date, nature of relationship to you, when possible, a social security number and the capacity in which he fits into the plan.

By this I mean to identify whether he is a beneficiary, or fiduciary.

I normally suggest that you first identify all of your family members. Then identify the persons whom you wish to serve as money managers for you or for your intended beneficiaries. Then identify your beneficiaries (even if you have previously listed them under the family members section).

If any of the intended beneficiaries have special circumstances, or if you wish to make special instructions regarding distributions to any specific beneficiary or class of beneficiaries, this is a good place to make that note.

Finally, specifically identify each of your assets, by type of property and state your appraisal of its value.

Categorize your assets by the following headings:

- Real estate;

- Depository accounts in banks, credit unions, etc.;

- Certificate stocks and bonds;

- Brokerage accounts;

- Mutual funds;

- Retirement plans (including IRAs, pensions, profit sharing plans, 401K plans, and deferred stock savings plans);

- Life insurance and annuities;

- Interests in businesses (whether closely held stock, partnership interest, or sole proprietorship);

- Motor vehicles; and

- Specially valued non-titled personalty.

I know. This seems exhaustive and exhausting to compile.

Let me give you a tip I always tell my clients when providing them with my standard financial disclosure form.

Use the form like an outline. Just list the name of each asset under the category listed.

Then, use the form as a list and provide me with a photocopy of each pertinent document which is attributable to each asset.

What I am really looking for is the document which best identifies the asset.

For depository accounts, brokerage accounts and mutual funds it is the most recent statement received. The same will usually hold true for IRAs.

For C.D.s, certificate stock or bonds and real estate, I want the title document itself. The same holds true for motor vehicles.

Life insurance and annuities; a copy of the policy.

Company provided retirement plan benefits: a summary plan description (the benefits booklet) and the annual participant's statement which comes out around the first of the year telling you the value of your employment benefits.

You must also provide the same information regarding your debts.

After all tax planning involves your net estate.

I have found that while clients usually have great difficulty preparing a financial disclosure statement in traditional form (most simply find it to be too much work); they can usually supply all of their financial information, using my method, in as little time as a week.

CONCLUSION:

In order to maximize the value of your estate planning conference, you must take a bit of time to organize the information your estate planning attorney will need. By taking the time to pull together the information described above, you will find your attorney can get right to the business of helping you protect yourself and your family in the most efficient and stress-free manner possible.

APPENDICES

Introduction

I have been attempting to write this book over the years and every time I just about had the topics discussed in the manner I thought appropriate, Congress or the state legislature would make some substantial change to more than one area of the law, such that major revision work was required. What appears below are chapters that were initially intended to be a central part of the main text. However, with the most recent estate tax law changes, these topics are no longer as pertinent to the average reader as they once were. As late as November of 2012, the estate tax threshold was scheduled to be $1,000,000 in 2013 and thereafter. In such an environment the discussions contained in this appendix would have been crucially important information for many readers to know .

However, with the most recent changes in the code raising the threshold for estate taxation to over

$5,000,000, it just didn't seem to me that all that many readers would be that interested in these topics, nor would they really need to know the information contained herein, as they might have in the past.

So, I have taken several chapters originally intended to be included in the middle of the book and placed them here. For those who are blessed with substantial wealth, you should definitely read these chapters. For mere mortals, if you are interested in the more sophisticated techniques that estate planners use to save clients literally millions of dollars, read on and enjoy.

I

Estate Taxation, The Basics

Historically, the structure of the estate tax code has remained the same since its inception: Definition of gross estate; Itemization of various deductions allowable, from time to time; Delineation of tax credits that may be available, again, from time to time.

It is this last area, the tax credit, which has been manipulated to compromise opposing political philosophies over the past decade or so.

A brief recent history:

In 2001, the now infamous Busch Tax Cuts were enacted by congress. Under this legislation, the minimum threshold for imposition of estate taxation rose from a then existing $675,000 to 3,500,00 in 2009; a repeal of the estate tax for the year 2010 (but a hidden increase in income tax for inherited assets) and a reversion to the law as it existed before the act was passed due to its "Sunset" Provision.

In similar fashion, the actual tax rates changed to be more lenient than under prior law. These provisions, too were covered by the Sunset Provision.

However, the sun never set, in actuality because before the sunset came a new dawn.

The new dawn came in the form of compromise legislation enacted by congress. Under this compromise the law did not revert to its previous condition. Instead of reversion to a minimum tax threshold of $1,000,000 the minimum was increased to $5,000,000 for the years 2010 and 2011 and $5,120,000 for 2012.

Again near the stroke of midnight, 2012, Congress again tinkered with the code. This time providing major taxpayer relief for the truly wealthy and, surprisingly, for many who believe that they constitute the middle class.

Instead of a reversion to the pre-2001 law, Congress increased the estate tax credit and established a maximum tax rate of 40% on those estates that are taxable. As an added benefit to taxpayers, Congress "indexed" the estate tax credit. This means that as the cost of living increases, so does the tax credit.

As discussed in Chapter Five, this means that in 2014 an individuals gross estate must exceed $5,340,000 before estate tax will be assessed.

As also discussed in Chapter Five, Congress also added a substantial benefit in the form of "portability". Portability, for the first time in the history of the estate tax law, allows a surviving spouse the benefit of the unused portion of the pre-deceasing spouse's estate tax credit, so long as he or she elects to do so by filing an estate tax return for the predeceased spouse's estate, whether one is otherwise required to be filed or not.

Notwithstanding the fact that most people will no longer be subject to estate tax as a result of the most recent congressional action, It still is not a bad idea to have a basic understanding of the estate code and the more common estate tax savings techniques.

Why?

Because Congress can giveth and Congress can taketh away.

With the current political emphasis on deficit reduction on both sides of the congressional aisles, a change in party control of the house could well see a reduction in the generous estate tax provisions by reversion to old standards.

With that out of the way, let's discuss the rudiments of the estate tax code.

The Estate Tax Code is technically divided into three subchapters: Estates of Citizens or Residents; Estates of Nonresidents not Citizens; and Miscellaneous. Our focus will be limited primarily to the first subchapter. Once again, this discussion is not intended, nor should be construed, to be an exhaustive analysis of the code. Such an analysis would be exhausting to both author and reader and is clearly beyond the scope of this work.

Rather, I hope to give you a very rudimentary understanding of the most basic principles encompassed in the code so that you can understand how the tax is assessed; how large it can be; and why the legal tax avoidance techniques described at various places in this book actually work.

First, it should be noted that both Gift Tax and Estate Tax are covered in the Estate Tax Code. These are called transfer taxes because the occurrence which triggers taxation is either the transfer without consideration (payment) in return from one living person to another (a gift), or the transfer without consideration in return which occurs as the result of the death of an individual. It is called a unified system because the tax brackets (as well as many other provisions) apply both to the gift tax and the estate tax.

The Unified Credit

As previously noted, the single greatest taxpayer benefit under the estate tax code is the unified credit.

Before one can understand this particular tax credit, one must first understand what constitutes a tax credit.

A tax credit is just what its name applies. After a determination is made of the amount of tax tentatively due; a subtraction from that tentative tax is made in the amount of any tax credits to which a taxpayer is entitled.

While an estate tax return is somewhat complex because of all of the schedules which display the various assets owned by a decedent at the time of his death, the technical structure of an estate tax return is quite similar to an income tax return.

```
    Gross Estate
 -  Allowable Deductions
    Adjusted Gross Estate

 x  Estate Tax Bracket
    Tentative Estate Tax
```

- **Available tax credits**
Estate Tax Due

It is important to understand the basic structure of the return in order to recognize one of those "common knowledge" mistakes which "everyone" commonly believes.

This piece of "common knowledge" is as follows:

The first $5,340,000 (in 2014) of value of every estate is exempt from estate taxation.

Under the most recent formulation of the law, this is, in fact a true statement because estate value in excess of this amount is subject to a flat tax of 40%.

However, it is still important to understand that this is a vagary of current law. Historically, estate tax, much like income tax, has been imposed under a system of escalating tax brackets. Prior to 2001, for example, the marginal rate was 19% and escalated to 55%. Under prior law, that contained escalating brackets, the fact that there was no exemption, but, instead, a tax credit, meant that the marginal bracket commenced with the first dollar owned at death not the first dollar after the exemption.

When this occurs the tax bracket on estates

of a size greater than the "asset equivalent value" of the tax credit (that's the $5,340,000 in 2014) will be taxed at an effective minimal rate far in excess of the marginal rate .

However, because the 2013 code revisions place a flat tax of 40% on estates of a value in excess of the asset equivalent value of the estate tax credit, the old "Conventional Wisdom" which was erroneous under prior law now actually is correct.

Nonetheless, I believe it important to understand how the estate tax code traditionally operated because, historically, when Congress makes changes in this tax code, it does so by tinkering with the numbers, not the template. And this is still the case with the most recent revision of the code, it's just a vagary that in so tinkering, by, placing the maximum tax bracket at the point where the credit leaves off, you end up with the "conventional wisdom" appearing to be correct.

Let's talk about the historic estate tax code template.

Under prior law, there was no exemption under the tax code.

What there was, however, is a tax credit. This unified tax credit (unified because it applies to both gift and estate taxation) is, to my knowledge, the only unequivocal benefit afforded by the estate tax code.

So, the way the system really works (looking at the formula set forth a few pages back) is that you compute the tax that is due on an estate by assessing the applicable tax bracket against the net estate found to exist after subtraction of allowable deductions from the individual's gross taxable estate, and only then does one subtract the applicable estate tax credit to find the actual tax due.

While under present law this may seem to be merely an intellectual distinction, I include it here in the discussion because if the law is changed to taxpayers' detriment in the future, this distinction will, once again, be important to anyone possibly subjected to escalating tax brackets. Remember, Congress is rarely "revolutionary" in tinkering with the estate tax code. Rather, it is evolutionary.

So if deficit concerns overwhelm conservative sentiment, this is an area where it would be very easy for Congress to raise taxes, just as it has used it to lower them in recent past.

The Marital Deduction

Among the deductions available both under existing law and existing law is the marital deduction.

In the past, this tax benefit can become a tax

trap for those who don't understand how the system operates.

Again, common knowledge inaccurately defines the marital deduction and its effect; this time as follows:

Anything which passes from one spouse to another either by gift or as a result of a transfer caused by death, passes from one spouse to the other estate tax free.

The truth of the matter is that in such circumstances the transfer does not pass estate tax free. Rather, it passes estate tax deferred. When does the deferral come to an end? It depends upon whether the surviving spouse is a United States citizen. If so, the deferral ends upon the surviving spouse's death. If the surviving spouse is not a United States citizen, the estate tax deferral ends much more quickly in time.

To the extent that the marital deduction allows a surviving spouse the use of all of the family's assets during his/her survivorship without diminution by estate taxes, the marital deduction is a benefit. However, in the context of family wealth transfer planning;

The Marital Deduction is an estate tax trap !

In order to understand why I characterize this deduction as a tax trap, look back at the structural skeleton of an estate tax return and ask yourself the following question:

If the full value of an individual's estate is removed from the estate tax return because everything qualifies for the marital deduction; of what value thereafter is the individual's unified estate tax credit ?

The answer, of course is :

Zero.

Again, while the most recent tax law changes makes this discussion concerning the marital deduction appear to be obsolete (because of portability); such is not the case for two reasons:

The marital deduction still plays a key role in "sophisticated tax planning for those still subject to the estate tax ;

Portability is only available to a surviving spouse who files an estate tax return on behalf of the pre-deceased spouse's estate, even if there is no requirement to file a return because the estate value is smaller than the asset equivalent value of the estate tax credit.

As a result of this "foible" of the new law, good estate planning attorneys are still integrating traditional "marital deduction" planning in estate plans for the truly wealthy. And the more conservative amongst us are still integrating such planning for clients with smaller estates as a precaution against Congress reducing the estate tax credit in future years, thereby subjecting even "modest" estates to taxation.

Returning to discussion where I left off with Zero:

What happens, then, when the citizen surviving spouse subsequently dies ?

Several things, in all probability, occur.

The estate grows. Absent estate tax planning the family's net asset value will probably be larger at the time of the death of the surviving spouse than it was at the time of the death of the first spouse to die because assets will probably continue to increase in value, either as a result of capital appreciation or additional unspent income.

A surviving spouse will ordinarily not dissipate the asset value of the estate. It is a sad fact that for most of us, regardless of the size of our assets, our fear of outliving our portfolio increases the longer we live. As a result of this fear, most people actually spend less as they grow older. Given that there is only one person consuming income or assets after the death of the first spouse, the family asset value tends to grow faster after the first death than before.

The usual estate tax problem we see in surviving spouses' estates, if they are taxable, is that they cannot give away the increasing value of the family's assets fast enough to keep pace with their growth in value.

The government is a longstanding institution. In the development of the estate tax code, the legislature has taken a patient, long term view of the taxation process. In that view, the loss of tax dollars received at the death of the first spouse is statistically more than offset by the increased taxation recouped upon the death of the surviving spouse; not only because of the increase in the estate's value; but far more importantly by that loss of the first spouse to die's unified tax credit.

When the surviving spouse later dies (let's assume shortly after the death of the first spouse so that we don't have to argue about the attainability of some hypothecated rate of return); the surviving spouse's estate contains the entire value of the family asset portfolio because the marital deduction, being of a value equal to the value of the gross estate, reduces the net estate to zero, leaving the first spouse to die's estate tax credit unused and forfeited.

CONCLUSION:

There is not much good news to be found in the Estate Tax Code. The only true good news is that everyone is entitled to an estate tax credit and the only thing you have to do to be entitled to it is die. While the marital deduction does provide additional funds for a surviving spouse's use; in the context of maximizing family wealth transfer, it is a tax trap. The good news in this regard is that with a little skillful planning, the trap can be reversed and you can benefit from the combination of the unified credit and the marital deduction.

Of course, now with "portablitity" this discussion appear obsolete.

However, the discussion still has value for the following reasons:

- ♦ A Democratic Congress that is concerned with budget deficits might well conclude to both reduce the value of the tax credit and once again establish escalating tax brackets. In such a case, the prior discussion would again be valid;

- ♦ Even if such an event does not occur,

conservative estate planners still utilize "A/B" planning in order to protect clients from their potential failure to elect portability on an otherwise needless IRC Form 706.

♦ The discussion of Marital deduction planning is still valid for married couples with exceptionally large estate.

II

THE MARITAL DEDUCTION TRUST AND MARITAL PLANNING

The solution to the problem just presented lies in that basic estate tax concept of incidences of ownership. In order for a transfer to qualify for the marital deduction, the surviving spouse must, as a result of the transfer, have obtained sufficient incidences of ownership. Conversely, if, after the completion of a transfer triggered by death, the surviving spouse does not obtain sufficient incidences of ownership over the asset in question, the transfer will not qualify for the marital deduction.

The problem presented in the last chapter resulted from the surviving spouse, at the time of the death of the first spouse to die, having obtained all of the incidences of ownership over all family assets as a result of the combination of how the assets were titled and the death designations (whether by beneficiary designation or Last Will) employed by the married couple. As a result, for estate tax purposes, all of the family asset value was removed from the estate tax return of the first spouse to die by deduction. As a result, the first spouse to die did not use his/her unified credit and the value of the credit was lost.

Suppose, however, there was a way to deprive the surviving spouse of sufficient incidences of ownership over some of the family assets, so as to avoid the marital deduction treatment, and yet still allow the surviving spouse virtually unfettered control over all of the family's assets. Before you get nervous about loss of control (assuming you think that you will be the surviving spouse) let's take a look at this technique and see, really, how much actual control of any asset is lost as a result of the technique. Remember when we talked about trust language and discussed the terms of the trust dealing with beneficiary designation ?

In our example when we discussed trust planning in the main chapters of this book the trust language said:

Upon the death of the first Settlor to die....the surviving Settlor/Trustee shall continue to manage the trust estate and administer it for the benefit of the surviving Settlor.

Upon the death of the first spouse to die, the trustee is directed to allocate and distribute the trust property into two separate shares, to be known as the Survivor's Trust and the family Trust.

> The Survivor's Trust shall consist of ½ of all of the trust property

Now let's add some estate tax planning language:

> less the value of all property passing to the surviving spouse other than by this trust;

> The Survivor's Trust shall also consist of all other trust assets having a value equal to the un- limited marital deduction, reduced by the following:

> All deductions, other than the marital deduction, actually allowed;

> The deduction allowed the deceased for state estate taxes.

> The amount needed to increase the deceased Settlor's taxable estate to the largest amount that after allowing for the unified credit against

estate tax, will result in the smallest tax being imposed upon the deceased Settlor's taxable estate.

All trust property not allocated and distributed to the Survivor's Trust Shall be distributed to the Family Trust.

Admittedly, even in a "watered down" state, the language dividing the trust assets at the death of the first spouse to die is complicated. Let's try to simplify the concept. At the time of the first Settlor's death the trustee is directed to divide the trust in half (conceptually, but not technically) to reflect each spouse's 1/2 ownership in the trust property.

Then the trustee adds to the Survivors Trust that amount of the deceased Settlor's share which exceeds the unified credit equivalent in existence at the time of the deceased Settlor's death.

Now let's talk about the terms of the "Survivor's Trust".

Believe it or not, even in the context of longstanding marriages (and almost universally in shorter term ones) spouses mutually are concerned that if they are the first to die, that their surviving spouse will find "someone new". This fear leads to a concern that the surviving spouse, if not restricted, will divert the survivor's share to that new someone to the detriment of the concerned spouse's children.

This concern is easily resolved through marital deduction planning, because the trust can provide that, while all of the income and the principal (if need be) can be used for the benefit of the surviving spouse, that spouse cannot re-designate alternate death beneficiaries. In other words, the residual benefit of the trust is locked in for the benefit of the children or other beneficiaries established in the original trust document. How does this occur? Let's look at the trust language to see.

The Survivor's Trust

The surviving Settlor, as Trustee, shall hold and administer the assets in the Survivor's Trust for the benefit of the surviving Settlor, as Beneficiary, as follows:

The Trustee shall distribute all of the income to the surviving Settlor;

The Trustee shall distribute principal to the surviving Settlor as the surviving Settlor may request, but only upon exhaustion of the principal contained in the Family Trust;

At the death of the surviving spouse, the Trustee shall distribute the then remaining property as more fully provided in the Family Trust. the surviving Settlor has directed.

As Trustee of the Survivor's Trust, the surviving spouse is granted the unfettered right of investment. As beneficiary, the surviving spouse, by the above language, is granted full benefit of the other three incidences of ownership.

By providing that the trust estate is divided upon the death of the first spouse to die according to a formula that allows maximum use of the first spouse to die's estate tax credit, and then placing minimal limits on the surviving spouse's ability to "tinker" with the beneficiaries, we do two things, protect the agreed upon beneficiaries AND insure that the predeceased spouse's taxable estate contains no more value than that of the asset equivalent value of the estate tax credit.

The "excess value" is shifted to the estate of the surviving spouse, to be covered by that taxpayers estate tax credit, instead of being subjected to estate taxation at the death of the first spouse, while insuring that the predeceased spouse's estate tax credit is not forfeited as a result of an overly broad disposition for the benefit of the surviving spouse.

Still with me?   Good!

But what about the terms of the Family Trust?

Good Question!

The terms of the Family Trust are different.

The surviving spouse is still the trustee, which means that he/she still has full investment control over all of the assets placed therein. However, the rights of the surviving spouse as beneficiary of the trust are substantially different from those provided in the Survivor's Trust.

The Family Trust

The trustee shall hold and administer the assets of the Family Trust as follows:

The Trustee shall distribute all of the income to the surviving spouse for as long as he/she shall live.

The Trustee, within the Trustee's sole discretion may distribute to the surviving Settlor so much of the principal as the Trustee deems proper, for the health, maintenance support and education of the surviving spouse in a manner consistent with such spouse's standard of living as experienced at the inception of this trust, for or any of Settlors' descendants.

At the death of the surviving spouse, the Trustee shall distribute the then remaining property among the Settlors' Descendants as the surviving Settlor has directed. If the surviving Settlor has made no such direction, the Trustee shall distribute the trust property as otherwise herein provided.

Now let's review how the incidences of ownership are affected by the terms of the family trust:

The surviving spouse, as Trustee, still has full power of investment of assets;

The surviving spouse, as beneficiary, still has the right to receive the income for consumer purposes:

The surviving spouse, as Trustee, has the discretion to allow the surviving spouse, as beneficiary, the use of principal for consumer purposes.

The Surviving Spouse's Power of Appointment, as surviving Settlor, is limited. The survivor can re-allocate among the previously designated beneficiaries but cannot add any new beneficiaries to the mix. Why? Because the power of appointment is limited to the descendants of the Settlors, the class for which provision has been previously made in the distribution provisions of the trust.

The surviving spouse's usual concerns:

While we have addressed the fears of the first spouse to die, what about the surviving spouse?

For some reason, the "surviving spouse" is usually worried about whether the principal of the trust is available after the death of the first spouse to die.

Let's go back for a moment and look at the spouse's right, as Trustee, to invade the principal for his/her benefit, as beneficiary.

Note that the exercise of discretion is limited.

In invading the principal the Trustee can do so only to the extent that the use of the principal by the beneficiary will support, but not exceed the standard of living experienced by the Settlors prior to the death of the first spouse to die.

Let's stop here for a moment and discuss these last two provisions. What the heck does each one really mean?

As regards the concept of the limitation of Trustee discretion of invasion of principal; I have found the simplest, most easily understood example to be with cars.

Let's suppose at the time of the first spouse's death, the husband drove a Ford Taurus and the wife drove a minivan. After one dies, the other wants to replace his/her vehicle which is now seven years old. For whatever reason, the surviving spouse wants to use the Family Trust fund to purchase a new car and the cost exceeds the income generated thereby.

What kind of car can be purchased?

If the survivor wants to buy a shiny red convertible (something he/she has always wanted) he will have to be satisfied with a Mustang. If, however, what the survivor is really looking to buy is that Ferrari of his/her dreams, he /she will have to purchase using principal from the Survivor's Trust, not the Family Trust; because the Ferrari is clearly beyond the means of living established during the time that husband and wife were both alive.

The question which is immediately asked after this explanation is as follows:

> If I am the Trustee, who's going to stop me from using the Family Trust in this manner ?

The answer of course is: "No one."

However, we explain, if the IRS finds out about this expenditure, because you have exceeded the limitations which the terms of the Family Trust placed upon you, as Trustee, you have exercised sufficient incidences of ownership over the assets in the Family Trust that they all qualify for marital deduction treatment. As a result, the IRS will go back and recast the deceased spouse's estate tax return as if all of the family's assets had qualified for the marital deduction at the time of such spouse's death, thereby destroying the tax planning which had been incorporated into the trust.

In short, if you violate the terms of the family trust you will obtain the same unfavorable estate tax result as if you had engaged in no tax planning whatsoever.

In the past, estate planners were so

concerned about this aspect of the trust that good practice dictated that the surviving spouse not serve as successor Trustee, alone. The fear was that having the power to actually invade principal, unchecked by any outside authority, would result in inclusion in the survivor's estate even though the totally unauthorized was never exercised.

In the last several years, the tax court has determined that there is no reason to believe that a surviving spouse, by innate nature, is a scofflaw. Thus, so long as the surviving spouse actually adheres to the limitations imposed by the Family Trusts terms, the family will be entitled to the favorable estate tax treatment afforded thereby.

Clients always ask the previously posed question.

I can never understand what motivates the question. If you really think about it, use of the Family Trust is the last thing that a right thinking surviving spouse would want to do.

Because the Family Trust assets are not includible in the surviving spouse's taxable estate, the next time the assets therein will be subjected to estate tax, after the death of the first spouse to die, is upon the death of the beneficiaries named to receive assets after the death of the surviving spouse.

In the meantime, those assets are all estate tax-free. This means that we can obtain one or even two generation's continued growth before the assets' values are reduced by estate taxes. Further, by splitting the assets among multiple beneficiaries (the Settlors' children or other descendants) the likelihood of later estate taxation can be reduced.

If the beneficiary's taxable estate is not large enough to sustain taxation at the time of such beneficiary's death (as a result of insufficient asset accumulation during the beneficiary's life or as a result of additional estate tax planning) estate tax may never again become due on the increased value of the assets therein.

On the other hand, the assets placed in the Survivor's Trust will most certainly be subjected to estate taxation at the death of the surviving spouse, if their value exceeds the unified credit equivalent value.

Thus the married couple who really understand how this estate tax savings technique operates will seek to reduce the Survivor's Trust's value, not the Family Trust, so that at the time of the surviving spouse's death, the Survivor's Trust's value is less than the credit equivalent value.

As regards the final power, the power of appointment, by limiting the surviving spouse's exercise of that power to a limited class of identifiable beneficiaries, the trust places sufficient limit upon the surviving Settlor's power of appointment that it, too, will be deemed an insufficient incidence of ownership to cause inclusion of the assets in the survivors taxable estate and will not be allowed marital deduction treatment.

By combining the last two limitations on the surviving spouse's power over assets in the Family Trust the assets are not included in the surviving spouse's taxable estate and do not qualify for marital deduction treatment.

Would limiting either incidence of ownership, alone, be sufficient to cause the exclusions which we seek?

No. It is the combination of limitations which cause the tax benefit.

Could we limit the surviving Settlor's incidences of ownership to a greater degree and still obtain the tax benefit?

At the death of the surviving Settlor, the Trustee shall distribute the then remaining property as the surviving Settlor has directed among the Settlors' descendants.

If the surviving Settlor has made no such

direction, the Trustee shall distribute the trust property as otherwise herein provided.

Yes. However, most spouses, when planning, are interested in minimal restrictions on the surviving spouse; probably because it is the usual circumstance that at the time of planning the order of death of the spouses is not accurately forecastable.

Assuming that the trust is drafted as provided above and the Settlors abide by its terms, what is the estate tax result?

By appropriately dividing the trust into 2 subtrusts at the death of the first's death and placing relatively minor restrictions on the surviving spouse's use of the Family Trust, substantial value can be taken away from taxing authorities and delivered to family members, instead.

And now for some questions from the audience:

In order to utilize this estate tax saving technique, does a joint trust have to be used?

No, in fact many tax practitioners frown upon the use of a joint trust and it is in your best interest to consult with a planner in your locality to determine if the use of a joint trust is warranted in your state. I have found that in states where the use of a joint trust is appropriate, clients tend to like to use a joint trust, rather than separate trusts, one for each spouse, with complimentary provisions.

The reason for this favoring is that use of a joint trust allows a deferral of the segregation of marital assets into separate trust shares until the time of the first spouse's death. Particularly in the Midwest, the notion of common ownership of assets by spouses (perhaps as a sign of marital fidelity) is commonly favored by clients. Further it is, as a practical matter, easier to manage a single trust portfolio.

What are the downsides to this trust plan?

Surprisingly, there are virtually no negative aspects to the plan.

The most common one cited is the fact that at the death of the first spouse the segregation of assets must occur and that, thereafter, there will be two income tax returns filed instead of one, one for the survivor on a form 1040 and one for the family trust on a form 1041.

Care must also be exercised to avoid the retention of current income in the family trust at year's end. This is because trust income is income taxed at a very unfavorable rate (39%) after a very small amount of income is retained ($8350). A wise trustee will usually distribute all of the income of the Family Trust to one or more beneficiaries to avoid this burdensome income tax rate.

For this reason, too, the well-advised trustee will tend to invest the assets in the Family Trust for capital appreciation, rather than generation of current income, while investing the Survivor's Trust for income rather than capital gain. The estate tax law mandates such investment of the Survivor's Trust assets (or, at the least, the surviving spouse's right to demand such investment by the trustee). My experience with clients after the first death of a spouse indicates that the most commonly heard complaint of the surviving spouse is there is not enough income generated. This is because most surviving spouse's, regardless of the value of the principal in the Survivor's Trust, are loathe to dissipate principal. Thus, maximization of income in the Survivor's Trust is usually an investment tactic favored by surviving spouses.

Other than as recited above, clients in my practice have not voiced complaints after the first death of a spouse. From this I conclude that most clients who have utilized this planning technique are fairly well-satisfied with the results.

Could this planning technique be utilized using a Last Will and Testament as the primary estate planning tool?

Yes, although then probate would not be avoided. It would be maximized. In order for each Will to have appropriate control, the division of assets by separate titling of 1/2 in the name of each spouse would have to occur before death. Otherwise, depending upon how title was held between the spouses, one of the two wills would never have affect. This means that there will be two probates and a maximum assessment of probate fees therein.

CONCLUSION:

Believe it or not, that was one of the simpler estate tax planning tools available to skilled estate planning attorneys.

Unfortunately, it is only available to married couples. There are additional estate planning techniques available which allow single individuals to reduce estate taxes where the value of their assets is in excess of the their unified credit equivalent and for married couples whose assets exceed in value their two credit equivalents. These additional techniques are not as easily explained as a marital deduction trust; so I shall leave their discussion to the next chapter.

III

SOME SOPHISTICATED ESTATE TAX PLANNING STRATEGIES

In the previous chapter I explained to you what is probably the most commonly used estate tax planning technique utilized by estate tax practitioners to cause estate tax savings for married couples.

What does one do if one is single and his/her portfolio is of a value which exceeds the unified credit equivalent value, or one is married and the family asset value exceeds the combined credit equivalent values ?

Unfortunately, there is no single answer to this question.

Sophisticated estate planning is as much an

art as it is a technical science. The tax practitioner must know the overall value of the portfolio, know the types of assets of which the portfolio consists and their component values. Further, the practitioner must understand which incidences of ownership are most important to the client. Finally, the practitioner must know the client's distributive intents. Once the practitioner understands all of these facets of the given client's situation, and only then, can he recommend to the client a comprehensive plan that will best serve the client's needs.

What I will not attempt in this appendix, is to describe a "complex" estate plan because there is no standard complex plan.

Instead, what I propose to provide in this appendix are descriptions of some of the more sophisticated planning techniques available to practitioners. My purpose in doing this is to provide the reader with some idea of how more sophisticated techniques work and to provide a "peek" at some of the tools available to estate planners to help clients legally avoid unnecessary estate taxation.

The Irrevocable Gifting Trust

An irrevocable trust is substantially different than a revocable living trust. Once the trust is executed, the terms of the trust cannot be changed and the trust itself cannot be revoked. Thus, great care must be taken when drafting such a trust because the client is going to have to abide by the terms of the trust, literally, for the rest of his life. Usually, but not always, an irrevocable trust will be drafted so that the IRS will consider the trust a different taxable entity for both income and estate tax purposes. This means that once the trust is executed and funded with assets, any income accrued in the trust according to its terms will be taxed at trust rates. These income tax rates are very disadvantageous. The marginal bracket is only 15%; however, the maximum bracket of 39% is imposed after accrual of only $8350 of income.

The benefit most usually sought to be obtained by the use of an irrevocable trust, is exclusion of an asset form the Settlor's taxable estate at the time of death.

How is it that the creation of the Irrevocable Trust takes and keeps an asset out of the Settlor's estate taxable estate?

The tax avoidance is created by the terms of the trust which severely limit certain incidences of ownership over the policy. They are as follows:

By virtue of the irrevocable nature of the trust, once created, the Settlor, thereafter loses his ability to alter the terms of the trust, thereby losing his power of appointment of the proceeds of the trust and; and

By the trust's terms, the Settlor will not directly participate in the enjoyment of the principal of the trust nor any of the income either.

So long as properly drafted, the Settlor can be the trustee of the trust and thereby retain investment control. However, if the Settlor is to be the trustee, great care must be utilized to restrict the usually broad investment and appointive powers of the trustee because some of the usual powers granted can be construed as providing some of the otherwise restricted incidences of ownership which must be restricted in order to keep the insurance value out of the Settlor's taxable estate.

Accordingly, it is usually the practice of most attorneys to require an independent trustee. In this way the attack of the IRS that the trust is a sham, meant only for improper estate tax avoidance can better be averted.

Funding the Irrevocable Trust

When utilizing an Irrevocable Trust care must be taken with regards to how contributions to the trust are made; so that the gift, itself, is not subject to gift taxation when made.

Even if the gift to such a trust is less than the $10,000 annual gift tax exclusion amount, the gift to the Irrevocable Trust will be gift taxable, unless a precise methodology is utilized in making the gift.

The reason that a specific methodology of gifting is required is because the gift to the trust is not a gift of a present interest. Rather it is a gift of a future interest to which the annual gift tax exclusion does not apply.

The gift tax annual exclusion (that one can give gifts which do not aggregate in value more than $10,000 in any calendar year) only applies to gifts of present interests. What is a present interest ? It is a confusing concept. (The law school of my attendance had a full semester course on the subject of future interests, which, of course is the opposite of a gift of present interest). However, I think that the simplest way to define a present interest is as follows:

A gift of a present interest is one where the recipient of the gift can enjoy the full benefit of the gift at the time at which it is given.

For example, if I give you five dollars today, immediately after the gift is made, you as the recipient can spend it, lend it, invest it etc.

A gift of a future interest, however, cannot be presently enjoyed. The beneficial aspects of the gift, by its terms can only be enjoyed sometime in the future.

An example:

If I contribute $5000 to an Irrevocable Trust and under its terms, the trustee is to invest the trust property until I die and then distribute the property and accrued income to my children; the enjoyment of the gift ($5000) is deferred in time to the future. My children cannot presently enjoy the benefit of the gift at the time it is made. Rather, they have to await my death before enjoyment can be had.

Since the contribution is a future interest, the annual gift exclusion does not apply. Accordingly, without more, a gift tax is due and payable whenever a contribution to the trust is made; the basis upon which the tax is computed being the value of the gift made to the trust.

Is there a way to prevent the imposition of gift tax upon the contribution to an irrevocable trust?

Of course there is; the provision for the utilization of a Crummey Power by the beneficiaries of the trust at the time that the gift is made.

Crummey Powers

The term Crummey is not meant to qualitate the power; rather, it is the name of the taxpayer whose court case established the acceptability of the use of the power about to be described as a gift tax avoidance technique.

The technique is relatively simple, although you would be amazed at how many people screw it up in application.

The purpose of the technique is to transform the future interest gift into a present interest gift which will therefore qualify for the annual gift tax exclusion. The technique is to provide for a limited period of time a present interest in the gift made to the trust.

This is accomplished by notifying the beneficiaries of the trust, at or near the time that a gift is made to the trust, that a gift has, in fact been made and that for a limited period of time (usually 15-45 days) the beneficiary has the right to demand, from the trustee, present distribution of his share of the gift. Because, if the demand is made, under the terms of the trust, the trustee is obligated to make the then present distribution of the proportionate share of the gift; the future enjoyment of the gift has been accelerated into a present, even if fleeting, possible enjoyment. This conversion, albeit brief in time, is sufficient to convert the future interest into a present one which can be (if in proper qualifying amount) gift tax free.

The IRS, when an Irrevocable trust is found to exist, will check to see if gift tax returns have been filed each year and will ask to see the notices which should have been provided to trust beneficiaries whenever gifts were made to the trust. If the notices and proof of their delivery to beneficiaries cannot be proven to the satisfaction of the IRS, it will go back and assess gift tax to each premium contribution.

As is the case with all sophisticated estate planning techniques, implementation and ongoing coordination of the estate plan should be conducted with the aid of a skilled estate planning practitioner.

Why make gifts to a Trust ?

Why not just make the Gifts to Individuals?

If the proposed beneficiaries are minors or young adults, the donor of the gift may not believe that it is in the beneficiary's best interest to give such beneficiary unfettered use of the asset. By making the gift to an irrevocable trust, the donor can still reduce his estate taxable estate by the value of the gift and yet prevent the young beneficiary from wasting the asset.

In the case of a married couple, a gift in trust is usually made so that, notwithstanding the gift, the couple can retain the enjoyment of the income generated by the asset in trust which would otherwise be denied them if the gift were made outright to the individual intended recipient.

An example:

A married couple has "family assets" of a total net value of $1,500,000 and, notwithstanding the increase in the unified credit to be experienced in future years, the couple believes that appreciation of the assets value will outgrow the credit increase. The couple wants to maximally benefit their children, but are not comfortable enough with the level of their wealth to wish to just "give away" substantial asset value at this time. Further, their children are relatively young and the couple believes that a gift directly to the children will only result in improper investment and loss, due to the children's lack of investment savvy at this time.

Instead of making gifts to the children directly, each establishes a trust for the benefit of the children, equally, and in the event that any of the children predeceases the surviving Settlor, then that predeceased child's share is transferred to his/her children (the Settlor's grandchildren) proportionately. In the event that at the time of the surviving Settlor's death a predeceased child is not survived by any descendants, then his/her then surviving spouse is entitled to distribution of the predeceased child's share.

There is an independent trustee appointed.

Further, it is provided that so long as each Settlor's spouse is alive, the trustee shall distribute to such spouse the income generated by the trust and that the independent trustee has a discretionary power of invasion of the principal of the trust to provide for the health, maintenance and support and education of the surviving spouse so long as said spouse remains alive.

As a result of these trust provisions, although each of the Settlors has no direct incidence of ownership over the income or principal of the trust, has no power of appointment of new beneficiaries after the trust creation, and has no direct investment control over the trust property or income; the Settlor does not have sufficient incidences of ownership over the assets gifted to the trust, to cause inclusion of the trust property in his/her own taxable estate.

Likewise, because the only incidence of ownership enjoyed by the Settlor's spouse is the right to receive the income generated by the trust principal, she/he has insufficient incidence of ownership over the other Settlor's trust to cause inclusion of its value in her/his taxable estate, as well.

So long as the independent trustee is cooperative to the wishes of each Settlor as regards investment strategy and invasion of principal for the other spouse; the net effect is that the married couple has, effectively, retained substantially complete beneficial use of the assets given to each's respective irrevocable gifting trust, while relieving the family of the tax obligation which would otherwise be imposed at the death of the Settlor or later death of his/her spouse.

What happens when one Settlor Spouse dies?

When the first spouse dies, the surviving spouse is denied the effective benefits of his/her own trust because he/she cannot experience those values and retain the estate tax benefit. In other words, because the non-Settlor spouse has died, the benefits afforded to her/him under the Settlor's Irrevocable Trust cease. As a result of this cessation, the Settlor Spouse is denied 1/2 of the benefits in the way of possible indirect enjoyment of income and principal of his trust which he/she experienced as a result of his/her co-habitation and cooperation of the now deceased spouse.

Are there any other reasons why donors would want to use a trust to make gifts rather than make gifts directly to the donees?

Of course.

Stacking Gifts for Favored Donees

It is usually the case (except in the case of very wealthy clients or clients who have wealthy children, a not uncommon estate planning phenomena) that the people whom the married couple really want to benefit is their children. It is only in the event of the child's untimely death, that the grandchildren or spouses become a direct target of benefit.

If gifts were made directly to the children, the limit of each parent's gifts in any year (assuming gift tax was sought to be avoided and the couple did not want to expend their respective unified credits in making the gifts gift tax free) would be $10,000 per child.

But, as a result of a tax court decision named after the taxpayer Cristofani, there is an additional benefit to making gifts irrevocably in trust. That benefit is that we are allowed, for gifting purposes, to stack gifts.

In other words I can make a gift to the trust on behalf of the contingent beneficiaries as well as the primary beneficiaries, even though, in all probability, the primary beneficiaries are the only ones who will relieve direct benefit from the trust.

The example:

Our previously described Settlors have four children, each of whom is married and has three children of his/her own.

As a result of the Cristofani Decision, each Settlor, in any given year, can make a total of twenty $10,000 gifts; one $10,000 gift for each child, grandchild and spouse; even though, in all probability the only people who will directly benefit from the creation of the trust are the respective children of the Settlors, assuming that each child survives the death of the surviving Settlor.

Thus, together, the spouses reduce family assets (for purposes of inclusion on their respective estate tax returns at the time of death) $400,000 per year ($200,000 [20x $10,000] each by gift to their respective gifting trusts) and so long as they are both alive, retain the income derived from investment of the funds in trust, and possible use of the principal, so long as the independent trustee so consents.

Where's the catch?

The only catch is in the annual gifting. Because the gift in trust is a future interest gift, in order to convert the gift into a present interest a "Crummey Right" must be extended to each beneficiary on whose account an annual gift is made, in order to avoid the imposition of gift tax on the transfer and the need to expend unified credit to cover the gift tax arising from the gift transaction.

When the Settlors' grandchildren are small, this will prove no problem, because the Settlors' children, as legal representative of their children can waive the exercise of the Crummey Power. However, after the Settlors' grandchildren attain majority (in Missouri, 18 years of age), the written notice of the Crummey Right must be made directly to the young adult. If the young adult exercises the Crummey power and Takes down his/her gift; the worst that the Settlors can do in the future is to avoid making gifts on account of the "greedy" grandchild. They cannot exclude the grandchild from participation in the trust, because the terms of the trust are irrevocable.

Great care must be taken not to explain the potentially adverse consequences of an exercise of a Crummey Right to potential gift beneficiaries. The IRS has taken the position that if a gift beneficiary waives the exercise of his/her Crummey right as a result of threat or by pre-agreement with the Settlors, directly or indirectly, then the right of exercise of the Crummey power is a sham and adverse tax consequences will result.

The irrevocable gifting trust, particularly in large families, can be a useful tool to reduce the size of the elder generation by asset value reduction while removing or lessening the sting (to the Settlor) of making the gift. By "stacking" the gifts, as aforesaid, the Settlor can substantially reduce the size of his/her/their taxable estate while restricting the enjoyment of the gifts in trust to their direct, primary intended beneficiaries.

The Irrevocable Life Insurance Trust

When an estate planner sees that there exists a substantial insurance value in a client's portfolio, the first inquiry of the client is for what purpose is the insurance.

Assuming that the purpose is other than providing "retirement benefits" for the client's use during his life (by borrowing against accumulated cash values in the policy during retirement and then letting the death value of the policy satisfy the outstanding loan value at his death), {not a bad retirement plan, by the way, for those who believe in the efficacy of life insurance as an investment}; one technique commonly utilized by estate planners is to create an Irrevocable Life Insurance Trust and cause the title ownership of the life insurance to be transferred to the trust.

Accordingly, the purpose of an Irrevocable Life Insurance Trust is to remove from the taxable estate of a Settlor and his spouse, if the Settlor is married, all of the value of the insurance deposited therein.

This technique works particularly well in the situation where the client wishes to purchase new insurance for a limited purpose (i.e.) to substitute for his earnings when critically needed, in case he dies while his children are all in college. The reason why the technique works particularly well with new purchases of term insurance is that new term insurance usually resolves the two adverse aspects of this planning technique:

Irrevocability; and

Settlor's need to survive the transfer of an existing policy to the trust by three years.

Let's talk about the latter disadvantage first.

Due to specific statutory provision, where the owner of the policy transfers ownership of a life insurance policy; in order to obtain the desired effect (the removal of the value of the policy from the owner's taxable estate) the transferring owner must survive the transfer of the policy by at least three years. Otherwise, notwithstanding the transfer, the death value of the policy will be included in the (now former) owner's taxable estate. It has to do with retained interests and it takes a long explanation which would only put most people to sleep. Trust me, this is what happens.

Thus, the funding of an insurance trust with a new policy which is purchased initially by the trust, will avoid the three year time delay of the effectiveness of the technique. the technique will have immediate affect.

Now, let's talk about the first aspect.

By using term insurance to fund an Irrevocable Life Insurance Trust, the disadvantage of Irrevocability can be avoided for so long as the Settlor of the trust is insurable and willing to pay term rates.

By utilizing a term policy, the Settlor can effectively revoke the trust merely by failing to pay the annual premium due for the continuation of the policy. Since the nature of term insurance is such that it only has value for so long as the insurance is in force, if the premium is not paid and the policy lapses, there is no value left in the insurance trust and the trust can be abandoned with no ill effect (other than the cost of creation of the trust).

I am not suggesting that one should willy-nilly lapse policies. This will be an expensive proposition. (I normally recommend the use of 10 or 20 year convertible term to blunt the annual increase in the premium and to allow conversion to a cash value insurance policy in the event that the Settlor experiences declines in health that would otherwise make him uninsurable).

However, by using term insurance, should the Settlor's dispositive desires change (he grows to hate one of his children, for example); even though the trust is Irrevocable, the Settlor, in effect, can revoke the trust merely by failing to pay the annual premium; and then create a new trust (and purchase new term insurance therein) to thereby change the provisions of the old trust which is now found to be less than useful by the Settlor.

In the usual Irrevocable Life Insurance Trust, the life insurance which is the subject of the trust, is not originally owned by the Settlor and transferred to the trust; because of that three year time deferral mentioned above. Instead, the Settlor transfers to the Trustee the amount of the premium, which the Trustee then utilizes to make the purchase of the life insurance policy initially in the trust's name. Thereafter,, gifts must be made to the trust in order to afford the trustee the ability to continue to pay the insurance premium and thereby retain value in the form of the death benefit in the trust.

Annuity Trusts and Qualified Residence Trusts

Some other handy, but more complex, planning tools are Irrevocable Trusts which are devised to give something back to the Settlor after he or she has made a gift to the trust.

Annuity Trusts offer a Settlor a method to give away a valuable asset at little gift tax cost while allowing the Settlor to continue to receive income generated by the gift for a limited number of years.

A GRAT (Grantor Retained Annuity Trust) involves a gift of a remainder interest in property which has little value (for gift tax purposes) because the Settlor retains the right to receive an annuity from the trust to which the gift is made

The Settlor creates an Irrevocable trust which provides that for a defined number of years, the Settlor will be entitled to receive an annuity (a yearly payment for a limited number of years). The amount of the annuity which the Settlor is to receive is determined by the term of years in which he will receive a payment and the IRS Section 7520 interest rates. When the annuity period ends, the Settlor has no more interest in the trust and the underlying assets which were gifted to the trust remain in trust or are distributed to other beneficiaries as are provided under the terms of the Irrevocable trust.

The value of the gift to the trust (for gift tax purposes) is only the value of the remainder interest, that is the value of the asset after reduction by the value of the Settlor's income right.

An Example:

Settlor transfers $1 million worth of bonds with a high yield or other investment asset that the Settlor believes will appreciate substantially in the short term. In return for this transfer the Settlor receives a two year annuity payment, the interest to be paid determined by the Federal Section 7520 rate (presently @ 1.6%).

Let's presume for our example that the interest or growth rate of the assets so transferred equals 10% per annum.

Here is what happens as a result of utilization of the grat.

Gift to Grat	1,000,000
Increase in value for year 1	100,000
Annuity paid at end of year 1	(512,000)
Value at end of year 1	588,000
Increase in value for year 2	58,800
Annuity paid at end of year 2	(512,000)

Value at end of grat   134,800

The play here is the difference between the Federal 7520 interest rate and the rate of return on the underlying assets contributed to the trust.

The larger the difference between the internal rate of return and the 7520 rate, the greater the value transferred to the intended beneficiaries.

Because the Settlor is receiving something in return for his transfer to the trust, the value of the "gift" to the trust is substantially less than the value of the asset transferred to the trust.

This is because the value of the gift is equal to the difference between the value of the assets contributed and the value of the annuity payments returned to the Settlor.

Thus when the trust is structured so that the initial gift is valued at close to zero there is little or no use of the Settlor's tax credit. If the Settlor survives the term of the trust, the assets then remaining in trust escape the Settlor's taxable estate at death.

This technique is of particular value to those of you who wish to benefit future generations but just can't get past the idea of giving up something you've worked so long to acquire.

Why?

Because this technique is particularly well suited to allow the transfer of future increase in value of an asset (whether by increase in value or as a result of income accretion).

So long as the appreciation in value of the assets contributed to the Grat is greater than the Section 7520 rate of interest, all that excess appreciation remains in the trust at its end, for the benefit of the chosen beneficiaries.

In case you are wondering, there are no adverse income tax consequences to these transfers back and forth.

The reason why is based in the structure of the Internal Revenue Code.

While most people think the code is a unified text that all relates together. Such is not the case. The income tax code was developed separately from the gift and estate tax code. As a result, there are "gaps" between the codes that allow savvy planners to take advantage of those gaps.

Thus, it is the case that for income tax purposes the income generated by an asset remains the Settlor's, for estate and gift tax purposes the asset generating the income is treated as not being included in the Settlor's asset base for gift and estate tax purposes. (More on this a bit later under the section of this chapter titled "Settlor Trusts").

Thus in the case of a grat, the trust can be structured in such a way that all of the income tax attributes of the assets transferred to the trust are still the Settlor's (it's as though the trust never existed) while the assets are truly conveyed away.

As a result of this gap there are no income tax consequences to the annuity payments to the Settlor. It is treated as if the asset is still titled in his name.

Even though irrevocable, an annuity trust is considered to be a SETTLOR trust for income tax purposes. This means that even if the trust generates more income than is required to pay the annuity, the entire amount of the income generated within the trust is income taxable to the Settlor.

This really isn't as bad as it sounds because to the extent that the "excess" income in the trust is taxed to the Settlor as if it were received, the tax paid by Settlor further reduces the value of his/her taxable estate, while allowing the unused income to accumulate inside the trust for the benefit for the remainder beneficiaries.

There is one catch to this technique, for the purpose of obtaining the estate tax consequence we want. The Settlor must outlive the term of the trust. This is as a result of estate tax laws regarding Retained Interests.

This concept of Retained Interest is really heady estate tax stuff. Once again, I'll not provide a complex, formal, accurate definition, but rather an inaccurate, practical explanation:

If at the time of the Settlor's death he/she retains any right to receive something back from the trust (the retained interest) the lesser of the trust property or the amount which is mathematically required in order tot provide the value retained, is includible in the Settlor's taxable estate.

This is one of the reasons why this technique is usually of a short term.

However, even if the Settlor does not outlive the term of years of the grat, the result is not disastrous. In such event all that happens is that the Settlor loses the cost of having the technique developed.

Other advantages:

Because the annuity payment will be greater than the income the contributed assets actually earn, the Settlor's income is not adversely affected during the term of the grat. If the grat is "zeroed out" the bulk, if not all, of the original asset value contributed to the trust is returned to the Settlor.

It really is a win/win for all concerned. The Settlor gets the return of his value contributed; the beneficiaries get the difference between the growth of the asset and the 7520 interest rate.

This technique is particularly appealing where one holds assets that have a good likelihood of substantial increase in value above the historically low 7520 rates.

High-yield bonds or publicly traded stock with upside potential are perfect for this technique.

What if the stock caps out and there is a fear that the value will fall? The trustee could sell the stock and invest in a substitute investment.

Or how about locking in that rate of return that has been experienced but may otherwise be lost? This could easily be accomplished by the Settlor substituting his promissory note with interest pegged at the rate of growth experienced by the capital asset to be transferred out of trust in consideration for the note.

Qualified Personal Residence Trusts

A personal residence trust is a special kind of GRAT.

In this GRAT, instead of gifting income producing properties, the Settlor's personal residence is conveyed to the trust subject to the right of the Settlor to remain in residence, rent free, for a given number of years.

QPRTs are a marvelous planning technique where the estate portfolio has disproportionate value in the clients personal residence.

The Mother of all Estate Planning Techniques:

The Family Limited Partnership

Suppose I told you that I could plan your estate in such a manner that you could retain all of the investment control over your assets, decide how much income to direct to yourself and how much to distribute to your intended beneficiaries each year; allow you reasonable (whatever the heck that means) use of principal for consumer use; and reduce the estate tax value of your estate by more than 1/3 before you made substantial gifts and reduced it for estate tax purposes even more by making gifts which would not overly interfere with the rights of investment control, personal use of income, or principal and over which you could add beneficiaries after creation of the planning tool and even reduce the size of inheritance of beneficiaries who subsequently gained your disfavor.

Would you be interested in utilizing such a tool?

For most readers with estate tax problems, I presume that your answer would be yes.

Well, the good news is that there is such a tool. The bad news is that, like every planning tool, there are some disadvantages to the planning technique.

The techniques is really an aggregation of techniques which, collectively, is called a Family Limited Partnership.

When I call this the Mother of All Planning Tools, I do not mean that all other tools find their geneses in this technique. Rather, I mean that this is the mother of all planning tools (as that term is often times used in references to Saddam Hussein). (Make your own joke here.) The recipe for this technique starts with a limited partnership. A limited partnership is, first of all a partnership, which is a group of people or entities who agree to place money or other things having value into a common enterprise, for profit, with an understanding that there shall be a proportionate sharing of profits and losses arising out of enterprise between them.

A limited partnership is a partnership composed of two different types of partners: the general partners, who under the terms of the agreement have the right to control the common enterprise and, as a result of such control, have unlimited personal liability for the actions of the enterprise; and the limited partners, who have virtually no control over the enterprise in which they have invested and, as a result of their lack of active participation in the enterprise, have a limit upon the amount of liability which can be imposed upon them as a result of the enterprise's operation by the general partners, the loss of their investment in the partnership.

Because the purchasers of limited partnership interests are, in essence, investing in the outcome of a venture, with virtually no control over the performance of the venture which, hopefully, will yield an increase value in the assets of the partnership which they are guaranteed of participating in only at the end of the partnership's term; the market, as well as the IRS view that only a fool would invest 100 cents on the underlying value of the partnership's assets in order to participate in the enterprise. Both the market and the IRS recognize that investors will only invest in this type of partnership at a discounted rate; when one takes into consideration the lack of control over the investment once value is invested and the lack of marketability of the interest in the partnership as a result of the terms against free transferability which are usually included in the limited partnership agreement.

How much discount in the value of an investment in the partnership is allowed by the IRS?

As usual, it depends upon the terms of the partnership agreement. Hence, it is essential that an estate planner well-versed in this planning technique draft the partnership agreement.

Who invests in this partnership?

Usually the Revocable Living Trusts of the Settlor Spouses who created the living trusts for probate and estate tax avoidance; described in Chapter 2.

The Settlor Trustees of Husband's and Wife's separate revocable trusts, each transfer substantially all of the assets in their respective trusts to the Limited Partnership in return for substantially all of the limited partnership units.

Who is the General Partner?

Because it is the case in nearly all states that if the position of general partner becomes vacant; the limited partnership is terminated; the general partner is usually either a corporation or Irrevocable trust of the planner's creation. I particularly prefer Irrevocable trusts in which the Settlor Spouses are the trustee's but in which they hold not interests in the income or principal of the trust. The downside to the use of such a trust is that once the trust is created and funded, the Settlors cannot change the alternate successor trustees nor can they change the beneficiaries of the trust. However, in view of the fact that the trust will most likely end shortly after the Settlor' deaths, as will the limited partnership, I am not overly concerned about this aspect.

The General Partner must have an interest in the partnership. However, even though the general partner, effectively, has all control over the assets in the partnership, its economic interest in the partnership is minimal, usually one per cent. This is because the purpose of the trustor corporate general partner is to allow a vehicle for the Settlors' control of the partnership during their respective lives; not retention of economic benefit.

The economic benefit of the partnership is held by the limited partners who initially hold (combined) 99% of the financial interest in the partnership. The limited partnership interests, as previously noted, are initially held by the Settlors of the revocable trusts, who, as trustees, have caused the investment of the trusts' assets into the limited partnership; from whence they continue to exercise investment control as the trustees of the irrevocable trust which has purchased the (minority) general partner interest.

Because the limited partners have no control and cannot freely transfer their limited partnership units, the value of the partnership units are discounted below the value of the assets within the limited partnership.

How big of a discount can one reasonably expect to receive?

It is not unusual for the IRS to consent to an assessment of a 20% discount for the lack of control and another 20% for the lack of free transferability. Combined, these discounts yield of 35% of the total value of the assets which have been invested in the limited partnership.

An example:

Husband and wife have family asset value of two million dollars ($2,000,000). Initially they each create separate Revocable Living Trusts and divide the family assets between them ($1,000,000 a piece).

Thereafter they cause to be created a Limited Partnership Of which an Irrevocable Trust of which they are the Trustees but in which they have no economic interest is the general partner. This trust invests its initial capitalization into the Limited

Partnership in return for a one percent interest in the partnership as general partner. Thereafter they, as co-trustees of the two revocable trusts, respectively transfer their assets in trust to the Limited Partnership in return for 49 1/2 interest in the partnership each, as limited partners.

If the partnership document is properly drafted, the Settlors can expect a discount in value, for estate tax purposes, in the value of each trust's assets, to the tune of 35%. This means that each trust, without further activity has an estate taxable value of $650,000. (under 1999 law)

Thus, if they both survive to the year 1999. (Remember I wrote this long ago.) Because the revocable Living Trusts have the marital tax planning described in Chapter 6, even though the fair market value of their family assets is $2,000,000; they will experience no estate tax value at either of their deaths that year.

Now let's make the estate planning pot a little bit sweeter. Suppose that each Settlor creates gifting trusts for the benefit of their children, as previously described in this overly long chapter; and utilizing the benefits of the Crummey and Cristofani court cases maximally contribute stacked discounted $10,000 gifts to the trusts; which in turn, provide that during the non-Settlor spouse's life, the income generated by the trust is paid by the trustee to the non-Settlor spouse.

With that provision in the Irrevocable Gifting Trust, even though the Settlors make gifts of limited partnership interests to the gifting trusts, they collectively still retain all of the income generated by the underling assets in the limited partnership.

Moreover, because the gifts are of limited partnership interests, instead of the underlying assets now in the partnership the value of the gifts are discounted for gift tax purposes as well as estate purposes. This means that when a gift valued at $10,000 of limited partnership interested is given to the Irrevocable Gifting Trust the real fair market value of the underlying asset value within the partnership has been discounted. Accordingly the $10,000 gift tax value is in actuality approximately $15,500 in real value.

Thus as gifts are made to the children's gifting trusts a disproportionate reduction in the value of the Settlors' taxable estates occurs.

It takes little imagination to see the estate tax savings value of this aggregation of techniques.

Additional substantial nontax benefit of this technique:

ASSET PROTECTION!!!!!!!

One of the unique attributes of a properly drafted limited partnership in all 50 states is that creditors may not levy directly against the limited partnership interests. At best, a judgment creditor can obtain what is called a charging order. This is a court order which allows the creditor to be substituted for the judgment debtor limited partnership. This means that the judgment creditor can receive the distributions which the limited partner, but for the charging order, would be entitled to receive.

Particularly where the partnership is structured to yield its income to the Settlors, the charging order is, generally, unappealing to the judgment creditor because, in practical terms, it avails him nothing. Further, in some cases, the imposition of a charging order can cause the forced surrender of the limited partnership interest which is its subject (although this has to be verrrrrry carefully structured to be effective and still yield the desired estate and gift tax savings).

Downsides:

Cost of creation

However when you look at the projected estate tax savings to be gained the cost of establishing the limited Partnership, the Irrevocable General Partner's Trust and the Irrevocable Gifting

Trusts for each child by each Settlor pales by comparison.

Increased maintenance costs

Remember the creation of all of these entities necessarily implies that each entity will be required to, at the least, file an income tax return each year in existence; and, if not carefully monitored, unpleasant income tax consequences can result. When you create this estate plan, it becomes a lifetime plan with lifetime maintenance costs. To the extent that there is going to be time delayed, structure gifting, there will be ongoing maintenance costs surrounding the utilization of the Crummey Power to secure the benefit of the annual gift exclusion for the gift in trust.

Loss of Stepped up Basis

Remember the trade-off benefit under the tax code for the submission of assets to the estate tax system at an owner's death is the step up in value of the asset for income tax purposes to the death beneficiaries.

However, when assets are held in a limited partnership, because it is the partnership units the value of which obtain the step up, the underlying assets within the partnership do not receive such benefit. Accordingly, it may not be advantageous to contribute low basis, high valued assets to a limited partnership because those contributed underlying assets will not obtain a stepped up basis at the death of the Settlors and the adverse income tax consequence will come to bear upon the intended beneficiaries. As is always the case in estate planning, careful, knowledgeable application of these and other estate planning tools must be made by trained estate tax practitioners in order to determine which planning tools, alone or in combination will yield the best overall benefit for your family's specific situation.

CONCLUSION:

In describing the various sophisticated estate planning tools included in this appendix, I have made no attempt to describe the techniques in a "technically correct" manner. Instead, I have tried to describe the techniques in a practical, easy to understand way which, in some cases, may actually be technically incorrect. I have included no sample forms for fear that the engineers among you will be tempted to adapt those forms yourself. Likewise, I strongly urge those of you who have been lulled into a false sense of security as to the ease of drafting or use of these various techniques to resist the temptation to seek forms and adapt them to your use. Nothing is more dangerous than an individual with a little bit of knowledge, only. There are many pitfalls laying in wait within forms which I have not discussed herein because my purpose in describing these techniques is only to let you see the "tip of the iceberg" as to the planning techniques available to a well skilled estate planning attorney.

ABOUT THE AUTHOR

JOSEPH R. BURCKE graduated from St. Louis University, A.B. Cum Laude, in 1972.

While at St. Louis University he was chosen to be a Congressional Intern, serving the late Congressman Melvin Price of Illinois. Mr. Burcke was awarded his Juris Doctor from the University of Missouri-Columbia in 1975.

He is admitted to practice before all state and federal courts in the state of Missouri as well as the United States Tax Court. He has represented clients in both federal and state courts, including the Missouri Court of Appeals and the Supreme Court of the state of Missouri.

A reformed litigator, Mr. Burcke's practice for many years has focused on the areas of estate planning and administration. He has spoken on such estate planning topics as "Living Trust Planning" "The Family Limited Partnership", "Tax Efficient Gifting Strategies" and "Planning for Your Adult Disabled Child" before numerous civic and private organizations, as well as at many public estate planning seminars.

He is a member of the Missouri Bar Probate and Trust Law Committee and has helped draft Missouri state law in the area trust administration. He also serves on the Missouri 21st Judicial Circuit Probate Court Committee.

He is a contributing editor to the ABA publication "The Special Needs Child and Divorce: A Practical Guide to Handling and Evaluating Cases"

In addition to his law practice and speaking schedules, Mr. Burcke is actively involved in his community. He has served as president and director of the Independence Through Employment Sheltered Workshop and as a director of the St. Louis Chapter of the Juvenile Diabetes Foundation and the St. Louis Chapter of the American Parkinson Disease Association and is a past director of Payback, a not-for-profit organization formed in association with the juvenile courts of the city and county of St. Louis, the purpose of which is to foster restorative justice for juvenile offenders.

He is the divorced father of two beautiful daughters, Meg, age 30, and Jill, age 25, upon whom he unashamedly dotes.

Printed in Great Britain
by Amazon